A December to Remember

Creating Christ-Centered Family Traditions

Carol J. Sonntag
& Alison R. Dunn

ISBN: 0692244387
ISBN 13: 9780692244388
Library of Congress Control Number: 2014918045
Basin Publishing, Ogden, UT

Contents

APPENDIX: STORIES **93**

"Christmas is what we make of it. Despite all the distractions, we can see to it that Christ is at the center of our celebration. If we have not already done so, we can establish Christmas traditions for ourselves and for our families which will help us capture and keep the spirit of Christ."

—THOMAS S. MONSON

INTRODUCTION

Imagine your family sitting together around a Christmas tree and talking about Christ, learning about His life, learning about love, sacrifice, and how to care for one another. Think about a young girl with a few dollars in her pocket, looking for someone in need. Think about a young family sifting through their clothes and toys for items that someone else may need more. Think of a young boy standing on a stool, trying to wash dishes to help his mom. Think back to your favorite memories of Christmas. Are they of gifts you received or gifts of sacrifice, time, and creativity?

Thinking about how to "...capture and keep the spirit of Christmas" is how this book began. *A December to Remember* stemmed from a desire to help my young grandchildren understand that Christ is the true gift of Christmas. So, instead of just buying toys that are soon discarded, I decided to replace them with gifts and experiences that would remind them of Christ.

Before December begins, I deliver to my children, all the books, stories, music, items, and gifts they will need for their month-long celebration of Christ. Each family is prepared to use their time in December to concentrate on Christ and how to become more like Him. My grandchildren and children have felt true joy as they have learned that giving is more rewarding than receiving. They have learned to embrace Christ and through practice have learned to become more like Him.

The excitement and joy that my grandchildren and children have had in opening these small gifts, looking for opportunities to serve others, and creating memorable experiences together, have turned this one-time project into a tradition. One daughter-in-law wrote in thank you:

"All of the thoughtful, carefully planned-out gifts you gave us this December helped prepare our hearts and minds to feel the Spirit of Christmas. It was price-less to have so many things to help our family, week after week, come unto our Savior during Christmas."

We have watched the excitement shift from Santa to Christ. Each family has adapted this tradition to the needs of their own family. It has grown and evolved over the years and, with the help of my daughter, has transformed into several different versions to meet the needs of many different families and individuals.

We invite you to join us as we learn, serve, and try to be more like Christ, and hope you make all of your Decembers: *A December to Remember.*

INSTRUCTIONS

HOW TO PREPARE:

- Start early. Use the preparation lists provided to guide your planning and shopping. Decide whether to use the Grandparent/Additional gift option.

- Make it personal. Add small inscriptions to the front cover of all the Christmas books, or consider writing your testimony of Christ in some of the books. Another option would be to record your voice reading one of the stories and include it along with the story or book.

- Gift wrap and label all items. We have found that gift bags work well for keeping all items for the day together and organized.

- Spend time as a family with the calendar. Write down all the activities that are already scheduled, intermixing *A December to Remember* days with your other holiday celebrations. One family divides each day into two days, due to the age and attention span of their young children. Think about what would work best for your family. Consider different time options, think about parents' work schedules, extracurricular activities, and bedtime schedules. Success comes from planning.

- Each book and story referenced in Part One has an annotation and description in the Reference section, so you can easily substitute other books and stories.

- Some of my favorite Christmas books are older and harder to find, so with these books, I have included another book or story. There are many used books available on the Internet. Almost all the used books I have ordered have been in great shape and quite inexpensive.

- Many of the stories referenced can be found online by doing a simple Internet search.

HOW TO BEGIN:

- Be flexible. With preparation and insight, you will find what works best for your family. Be prepared to modify the books, stories, and challenges/activities for your own family. On busy days, choose a character or challenge/activity that requires less time.

- Look for ways to involve the children. Pick a child to be in charge of distributing or opening gifts each day. Also, involve them in singing the songs and reading the books or stories.

- If you are using a Nativity option, open the Nativity figure first, so it can be the focus of the music, story, and activity.

- Spend time talking about the results of the challenges, especially with your older children, and ask them what they did, how they felt, and if they noticed a change in themselves or others.

- Create room for Christ. Make room for your children to find Him throughout December!

PART ONE

Nativity-Centered Traditions

"At the focal point of all human history, a point illuminated by a new star in the heavens revealed for just such a purpose, probably no other mortal watched— none but a poor young carpenter, a beautiful virgin mother, and silent stabled animals who had not the power to utter the sacredness they had seen. Shepherds would soon arrive and later, wise men from the East. Later yet the memory of that night would bring Santa Claus and Frosty and Rudolph—and all would be welcome. But first and forever there was just a little family, without toys or trees or tinsel. With a baby—that's how Christmas began. It is for this baby that we shout in chorus: 'Hark! The herald angels sing, Glory to the newborn King!...Mild he lays his glory by, Born that man no more may die; Born to raise the sons of earth, Born to give them second birth."

—JEFFREY R. HOLLAND

ORIGINAL FAMILY VERSION

The focus of this version is the Nativity. The people and animals present at the birth of Christ are highlighted for each day. The books suggested are illustrated children's books. The short stories are mostly from, *The Friend*, or printed in the Appendix. All books and stories are included in the annotated Reference section. The activities and challenges are planned to do together as a family and will give opportunities to become more like the Savior.

Other Suggestions: Choose a Nativity set that is child-friendly, and consider wood, so it can be touched, reverenced, and used in dramatic play all month. Wrap all gifts and place in a gift bag labeled for each Nativity character. All music for this version is from the *Children's Songbook* or *Children's Songbook CD of the Church of Jesus Christ of Latter-day Saints*.

MANGER

- **Gifts:** Manger, doll, straw (raffia)
- **Music:** "Away in a Manger," pg. 42, disc #1, song 44, *Children's Songbook*
- **Story:** "Straw For the Manger," Jacob F. Frandsen
- **Challenge/Activity:** Every time you do something for the Savior (anything nice you do for someone else without being asked), put a piece of "straw" in the manger. Try to have enough straw in the manger by Christmas Day to make a comfortable bed for Baby Jesus. The Manger could be a purchased manger, box, or construct the manger included in the Additional Resources
- **Grandparent/Additional Gift Option:** Construct a manger, make a doll, and cut raffia for the straw (instructions in Additional Resources)

MARY

- **Gift:** Mary
- **Music:** "Mary's Lullaby," pg. 44, disc #1, song 45
- **Book:** *Why Christmas Trees Aren't Perfect*, Richard H. Schneider
- **Challenge/Activity:** Write a note to your mom, thanking her for all she does for you. Find a special time to give it to her.
- **Grandparent/Additional Gift Option:** A gift for your children to give their mother would be an appreciated addition. It could be anything you think your daughter or daughter-in-law would like. Consider the book *Mary, the Mother of Jesus* by Camille Fronk Olson. My grandchildren loved wrapping "their" gift with the gift-wrapping supplies I included.

JOSEPH

- **Gifts:** Joseph, Nativity Flannel Board Set
- **Music:** "When Joseph Went to Bethlehem," pg. 47, disc # 1, song 39
- **Watch:** "Joseph and Mary Travel to Bethlehem," *The Life of Jesus Christ—Bible Videos*, lds.org
- **Challenge/Activity:** Tell the events that occurred at Jesus Christ's birth with flannel board figures.
- **Grandparent/Additional Gift Option:** Nativity Flannel Board Set and a flannel board.

DONKEY

- **Gift:** Donkey
- **Music:** "Christmas Bells," pg. 54, disc #2, song 1
- **Watch:** DVD, *The Little One*, Pamela Reid
- **Challenge/Activity:** Find a way to be kind to an animal today. If you don't have animals or a pet, feed the birds or ducks.
- **Grandparent/Additional Gift Option:** Bird feeder and seed

FIRST WISE MAN

- **Gift:** Wise Man
- **Music:** "Picture A Christmas," pg. 50, disc #1, song 49
- **Book:** *The Carpenter's Gift*, David Rubel
- **Challenge/Activity:** Make a Christmas treat for another family. Deliver it by sneaking the treat to their front door, ringing the doorbell, and running away, so they will not know who brought the surprise.
- **Grandparent/Additional Gift Option:** Make or purchase a brownie/cookie mix that the family could make together.

SECOND WISE MAN

- **Gifts:** Wise Man, envelope containing money
- **Music:** "Sleep, Little Jesus," pg. 47, disc #1, song 47
- **Book:** *Christmas Train*, Thomas S. Monson
- **Challenge/Activity:** Open the envelope containing a one-dollar bill for each family member. Use this money, plus any of your own resources, to make life better for someone else.
  - » Examples:
    - ○ Have every family member earn or add some money to the included money, and donate the total to someone in need or a local shelter or charity.
    - ○ Buy ingredients or supplies, and make something to give to someone in need.
    - ○ Buy food or requested items for a local shelter.
- **Grandparent/Additional Gift Option:** Provide the envelope and money

THIRD WISE MAN

- **Gift:** Wise Man
- **Music:** "Who Is This Child?" pg. 46, disc #1, song 46
- **Book:** *The Tale of the Three Trees: A Traditional Folktale,* Retold by Angela Elwell Hunt
- **Challenge/Activity:** Make three Christmas ornaments. Give away or use them to decorate for Christmas.
- **Grandparent/Additional Gift Option:** Craft supplies/kit for ornaments

CAMEL

- **Gift:** Camel
- **Music:** "Picture a Christmas," pg. 50, disc # 1, song 49
- **Story:** "The Littlest Camel" (Appendix)
- **Challenge/Activity:** Have each child draw a picture to illustrate the story. When illustrations are finished, reread the story using the illustrations.
- **Grandparent/Additional Gift Option:** Storyboard (instructions in Appendix), paper, markers, vinyl sheets, and rings. This has been a fun tradition to add illustrations each year and watch their artistic talents develop. Putting their illustrations in vinyl sheets and attaching them to the storyboard with rings preserves them for years. My grandchildren like to see the pictures their parents drew.

SHEPHERD

- **Gifts:** Shepherd, candy canes
- **Music:** "The Shepherd's Carol," pg. 40, disc #1, song 42
- **Book:** *The Little Shepherd's Christmas*, Carol Heyer
- **Challenge/Activity:** Open the box of candy canes, and divide them so each child has at least two candy canes. One candy cane will be for them, and the other candy cane they can share with a friend. Talk about whom they would like to give their candy cane to and why they think that would be a good choice.

LAMB

- **Gift:** Lamb
- **Music:** "Stars Were Gleaming," pg. 37, disc #1, song 38
- **Read:** *The Crippled Lamb*, Max Lucado
- **Challenge/Activity:** Today, have each member of the family look for an individual that they could help in some way. Share your experiences.
- **Grandparent/Additional Gift Option:** Pajamas for each child

BABY JESUS

- **Gift:** Baby Jesus from Nativity
- **Music:** "Little Jesus," pg. 39, disc #1, song 40
- **Read:** Luke 2: 1-20, Matthew 2: 1-12
- **Challenge/Activity:** Display a picture of Christ while you discuss what you have learned about Jesus Christ and how you have honored Him this December.
- **Grandparent/Additional Gift Option:** A framed picture of Jesus Christ

STABLE OPTION

STABLE:

- **Gift:** Stable (if included in set)
- **Music:** "Once Within a Lowly Stable," pg. 41, disc #1, song 43
- **Challenge/Activity:** Retell the story of Jesus's birth using all the characters in your Nativity set.
- **Grandparent/Additional Gift Option:** *The Story of Christmas Activity Book* or other Nativity activity book

CLASSIC CHILDREN'S LITERATURE

I love children's Christmas books, so this version is organized around some of my favorite Christmas books. All the books, stories, and challenges/activities are unique to this version, but if you especially liked some of the suggested books, stories, challenges/activities from another version or your own favorites, substitute them.

You may want to re-use a Nativity set and wrap the characters for this December or give a new Nativity. All Christmas songs listed in this version are from the *Children's Songbook or CD of The Church of Jesus Christ of Latter-day Saints.*

MANGER

- **Gifts:** Manger from Nativity set, straw & and manger from the Original version
- **Music:** "The Nativity Song," pg. 52, disc #2, song 1
- **Book:** Luke 2:1-20 and Matthew 2:1-12
- **Challenge/Activity:** Introduce the manger project from last year. Remember to add a piece of straw to the manger every time you do something for the Savior (anything nice you do for someone else without being asked). Try to have enough straw in the manger by Christmas Day to make a comfortable bed for Baby Jesus.
- **Grandparent/Additional Gift Option:** A Nativity book with the text from the Bible, I like: *The Story of Christmas from the King James Bible,* illustrated by Pamela Dalton.

NATIVITY-CENTERED TRADITIONS

ANGEL

- **Gift:** Angel
- **Music:** "Stars Were Gleaming," pg. 37, disc #1, song 38
- **Book:** *This Is the Stable,* Cynthia Cotton
- **Challenge/Activity:** Do something "angelic" for someone
- **Grandparent/Additional Gift Option:** If the Nativity set does not include an angel, purchase a separate angel. I chose to add a white porcelain angel with a small battery candle, which became a favorite of my grandchildren.

MARY

- **Gift:** Mary
- **Music:** "The Shepherd's Carol," pg. 40, disc #1, song 42
- **Book:** *The Year of the Perfect Christmas Tree*, Gloria Houston
- **Challenge/Activity:** Play the "Christmas Box of Questions," or make up your own questions, i.e., "What is the most memorable Christmas gift you have ever given?" or "What are you looking forward to this Christmas?"
- **Grandparent/Additional Gift Option:** "Christmas Box of Questions Game, Melissa and Doug"

JOSEPH

- **Gift:** Joseph
- **Music:** "Picture a Christmas," pg. 50, disc #1, song 49
- **Book:** *Christmas Day in the Morning*, Pearl S. Buck
- **Challenge/Activity:** Surprise your dad, like Rob did, by doing something to help him (shovel the sidewalk, take out the garbage, wash the car, etc.).

NATIVITY-CENTERED TRADITIONS

DONKEY

- **Gift:** Donkey
- **Music:** "When Joseph Went to Bethlehem," pg. 47, disc #1, song 39
- **Book:** *Mr. Willowby's Christmas*, Robert Barry
- **Challenge/Activity:** Invite someone in your family to use something of yours that you usually don't let them use.

SHEPHERD

- **Gift:** Shepherd
- **Music:** "There Was Starlight on the Hillside," pg. 40, disc #1, song 41
- **Book:** *There Was No Snow on Christmas Eve*, Pam Munoz Ryan
- **Challenge/Activity:** Make snowflakes. Decorate a window with your snowflakes for another person, such as a nursing home resident or another person who needs cheering.
- **Grandparent/Additional Gift Option:** Pipe cleaners, borax and string for making snowflakes (instructions in Additional Resources)

FIRST WISE MAN

- **Gift:** Wise Man
- **Music:** "Sleep, Little Jesus," pg. 47, disc #1, song 40
- **Book:** *Christmas Miracle of Jonathan Toomey*, Susan Wojciechowski
- **Challenge/Activity**: The Wise Men gave gifts to Baby Jesus, so give your own gift to Jesus by giving something of yours away. Think about what you could give to another child in need: toys, books, or clothes. Choose a time to deliver your things to an agency, shelter, or individual.

SECOND WISE MAN

- **Gift:** Wise Man
- **Music:** "Christmas Bells," pg. 54, disc #2, song 2
- **Book:** *The Gingerbread Doll*, Susan Tews or *Christmas Tapestry*, Patricia Polacco
- **Challenge/Activity:** Make gingerbread cookies and share them.
- **Grandparent/Additional Gift Option:** A gingerbread cookie/house kit

CAMEL

- **Gift:** Camel
- **Music:** "Once within a Lowly Stable," pg. 41, disc #1, song 43
- **Book:** *The Christmas Star*, Marcus Pfister
- **Challenge/Activity:** Take some time to go outside after dark with sleeping bags or blankets, and stare at the stars. Think of that silent night long ago.

THIRD WISE MAN

- **Gift:** Wise Man
- **Music:** "Oh, Hush Thee, My Baby," pg. 48, disc #1, song 48
- **Book:** *The Man of the House at Huffington Row*, Mary Brigid Barrett or *The Little Fir Tree*, Margaret Wise Brown
- **Challenge/Activity:** Give away something you create, or share one of your talents with someone (sculpt something, draw a picture, do a dance, play, or sing a song, etc.).

LAMB

- **Gift:** Lamb
- **Music:** "Who Is the Child?" pg. 46, disc #1, song 46
- **Book:** *Santa's Favorite Story: Santa Tells the Story of the First Christmas*, Husako Aoki
- **Challenge/Activity:** Have each family member earn money to purchase socks to donate to an agency collecting new socks, or choose someone you know who would be blessed by your anonymous gift of socks.
- **Grandparent/Additional Gift Option:** "Warm and wooly" socks for each family member   .

BABY JESUS

- **Gift:** Baby Jesus from Nativity set
- **Music:** "Away in a Manger," pg. 42, disc #1, song 44
- **Challenge/Activity:** Have each member of your family share their favorite scripture or story of Christ.

COSTUME VERSION

This Nativity-Centered version uses costumes for each character. You could use the costumes with or without the gift of a Nativity figure, as used in previous years. Children love dramatic play, so they will have fun pretending to be all the people and animals present at Jesus's birth. Feel free to combine costumes and characters in any way that works for your family. Music is from the *Children's Songbook or CD of the Church of Jesus Christ of Latter-day Saints*.

Use the Manger and straw challenge activity as outlined in the Original and Classic Literature versions or use the "sparkle box," included in the book *The Sparkle Box*, as your family's incentive to help others this December.

Other Suggestions: Instead of costumes, use puppets.

ANGEL

- **Gift:** Angel costume and/or angel figure
- **Watch:** "An Angel Foretells Christ's Birth to Mary," *The Life of Jesus Christ—Bible Videos*, lds.org
- **Book:** *Storybook Set and Advent Calendar*, retold by Mary Packard, consisting of twenty-four miniature books arranged in sequence and retelling the story of Christ's birth, along with an advent calendar
- **Grandparent/Additional Gift Option:** Provide a small Christmas tree for all the ornaments/books.

MARY

- **Gift:** Mary costume
- **Music:** "Oh, Hush Thee, My Baby," pg. 48, disc #1, song 48
- **Book:** *The Nativity Mary Remembers*, Laurie Knowlton or "Two Dimes and a Nickel," Richard A. Robb
- **Challenge/Activity:** Do a secret act of kindness for your mom, or help her with one of her many responsibilities.
- **Grandparent/Additional Gift Option:** A restaurant gift card for your mom, so she can have a day off from preparing dinner sometime this month.

JOSEPH

- **Gift:** Joseph costume
- **Music:** "When Joseph Went to Bethlehem," pg. 38, disc #1, song 39
- **Watch:** DVD, *Christmas for a Dollar*, Gale Sears (also available as a book)
- **Challenge/Activity:** Make a treat for dad. Eat it together while watching the DVD or reading the book.
- **Grandparent/Additional Gift Option:** Dad's favorite treat

DONKEY

- **Gift:** Donkey costume or a prop that could be used for a donkey
- **Music:** "Christmas Bells," pg. 54, disc #2, song 2
- **Book:** *The Little Donkey*, Gerda Marie Scheidl, or *Christmas Farm*, Mary Lyn Ray
- **Challenge/Activity**: Have each family member make a gratitude list. List all the people who have encouraged you during this past year, then write at least one "thank you" note to express your gratitude to one of the people you listed.
- **Grandparent/Additional Gift Option:** "Thank you" note cards and stamps

FIRST WISE MAN

- **Gift:** Wise man costume
- **Music:** "Have a Very Merry Christmas," pg. 51, disc #1, song 50
- **Book:** *An Orange for Frankie*, Patricia Polacco
- **Challenge/Activity**: Collect gently used hats/gloves/coats and donate to a homeless shelter or to someone who needs warm winter clothes. Try to make your gift anonymous.
- **Grandparent/Additional Gift Option:** Hats, gloves, and coats to add to their donation

CAMEL

- **Gift:** Camel costume or a prop that could be used for a camel
- **Music:** "Once within a Lowly Stable," pg. 41, disc #1, song 43
- **Book:** *The Last Straw*, Fredrick H. Thury
- **Challenge/Activity:** Think of things you can carry to help members of your family. Have fun carrying things for others without being asked.

SECOND WISE MAN

- **Gift:** Wise man costume
- **Music:** "Stars Were Gleaming," pg. 37, disc #1, song 38
- **Book:** *Dressing-Up Sticker Book: Nativity Play*, illustrated by Kay Widdowson, or other Nativity sticker book
- **Challenge/Activity**: Stick your stickers into your book, and tell the story of Jesus's birth (you may take several days to complete your book.)
- **Grandparent/Additional Gift Option**: Sticker books

THIRD WISE MAN

- **Gift:** Wise Man costume
- **Music:** "Picture a Christmas," pg. 50, disc #1, song 49
- **Story:** "Doll Brings Lesson on Christmas," Adrianna Cabello
- **Challenge/Activity**: Give away one of your dolls or stuffed animals to someone or some agency in need of children's toys.
- **Grandparent/Additional Gift Option:** A simple doll or stuffed animal sewing kit that your grandchildren can complete and give away

SHEPHERD

- **Gift:** Shepherd costume
- **Music:** "The Shepherd's Carol," pg. 40, disc #1, song 42
- **Book:** *The Little Shepherd Girl*, Julianne Henry
- **Challenge/Activity**: Give away something that cannot be bought.
  - Smile at someone
  - Give someone a compliment (say something nice)
  - Give someone a hug

LAMB

- **Gift:** Lamb costume or prop that could be used as a lamb
- **Music:** "Who Is This Child?" p 46, disc #1, song 46
- **Book:** *The Scallop Christmas,* Jane Freeberg
- **Challenge/Activity:** Make fleece blankets and give them to a care center, hospital or shelter. Project Linus is another great option @ projectlinus.org.
- **Grandparent/Additional Gift Option:** Purchase fleece and cut into blanket sizes. Have children cut and finish edges.

BABY JESUS

- **Gift:** "Swaddling clothes" for a doll representing Baby Jesus
- **Music:** "Beautiful Savior," pg. 62, disc #2, song 11
- **Challenge/Activity:** Present a Christmas Nativity play using all your costumes and props. Invite extended family or friends, so you will have enough actors to play all the parts and an audience. Have the narrator read Luke 2:1-20 and Matthew 2:1-12.
- **Grandparent Option:** Help with the Nativity play, or be part of the exuberant audience.

TRADITIONAL CHRISTMAS CAROL VERSION

"Music is definitely one of the easiest ways to focus Christmas on our Savior. The kids took turns choosing the songs—deciding according to which of the beautiful artwork struck their fancy that night. We talked about traditions depicted in the illustrations, or about the meaning in the words of the songs. Enjoying this book throughout December will always be a treasured tradition in our home."
—MARIANNE SONNTAG, MY DAUGHTER-IN-LAW

Traditional Christmas carols are highlighted in this version. Select a songbook to use all month, based on the musical abilities of your family. The goal is to have your children learn and memorize some traditional Christmas carols. Let your children accompany or lead the Christmas carols you sing each night. Since this version emphasizes music, spend extra time each night learning a Christmas carol and singing together. I have suggested a Christmas carol for each Nativity character, but you could also take turns having family members choose their favorite Christmas carol.

Grandparent/Additional Gift Options: Bells and/or chimes would make a fun addition to this version. Another gift could be a Christmas songbook.

STABLE
- **Gift:** Stable (if included)
- **Music:** "Away in a Manger"
- **Book:** *Away in a Manger*, Mike Jaroszko
- **Challenge/Activity:** Have each family member clean one room of your stable (house)

MARY

- **Gift:** Mary
- **Music:** "Silent Night"
- **Book:** *Gifts of the Heart*, Patricia Polacco
- **Challenge/Activity:** Find some way to show your appreciation for someone who serves you, i.e., teachers, leaders, coaches, babysitters, etc.

DONKEY

- **Gift:** Donkey
- **Watch:** YouTube videos: "The Friendly Beasts: Brian Stokes Mitchell with the Mormon Tabernacle Choir" and/or "Ethan Illustrates One of His Favorite Stories"
- **Book:** *The Friendly Beasts*, Tomie dePaola
- **Music:** "The Friendly Beasts"
- **Challenge/Activity:** Sometimes the donkey that carried Mary is described as a "gentle" donkey. Do something gentle for someone today.

COW

- **Gifts:** Cow, sticker book
- **Music:** "O Little Town of Bethlehem"
- **Book:** *The Boy of the Bells*, Carly Simon, or *Jacob's Gift*, Max Lucado
- **Challenge/Activity:** Spend time together playing and singing Christmas carols
- **Grandparent/Additional Gift Option:** Musical instruments—consider a set of bells or chimes. You could even make your own set of pipe chimes (instructions available online).

JOSEPH

- **Gift**: Joseph
- **Music:** "God Rest Ye, Merry Gentlemen"
- **Story:** "A Helping Angel," Mary Joanne Sreck Steck
- **Challenge/Activity:** Today, do at least one nice thing for Dad.
- **Grandparent/Additional Gift Option:** Give your grandchildren a gift to give their dad (car wash gift card, sporting goods gift card, etc.)

FIRST WISE MAN

- **Gift:** Wise Man
- **Book:** *We Three Kings,* illustrated by Gennady Spirin
- **Music:** "We Three Kings"
- **Challenge/Activity:** Donate some of your books to a homeless shelter, day-care center, or other agency in need of books.
- **Grandparent/Additional Gift Option:** Additional books for your grandchildren to donate

SECOND WISE MAN

- **Gifts:** Wise Man and Christmas candy
- **Music:** "Hark! The Herald Angels Sing"
- **Watch:** "The Wise Men Seek Jesus," *The Life of Jesus Christ—Bible Videos,* lds.org
- **Challenge/Activity:** Enjoy some of this Christmas candy, share the rest with someone who needs to be remembered or included.
- **Grandparent/Additional Gift Option:** Homemade Christmas treats

THIRD WISE MAN

- **Gift:** Wise Man
- **Book:** *The First Noel*, illustrated by Jody Wheeler
- **Music:** "The First Noel"
- **Challenge/Activity:** Go Caroling to people who would appreciate your gift.
- **Grandparent/Additional Gift Option:** Hot chocolate mix or a gift card for going out for hot chocolate after caroling

CAMEL

- **Gift:** Camel
- **Book:** *Good King Wenceslas*, illustrated by Omar Rayyan
- **Music:** "Good King Wenceslas"
- **Challenge/Activity:** Do a secret act of kindness for someone today.

SHEPHERD

- **Gift:** Shepherd
- **Book:** *The Little Drummer Boy*, Ezra Jack Keats
- **Music:** "The Little Drummer Boy" (if found in the back of your copy of *The Little Drummer Boy*)
- **Challenge/Activity:** Gather items that could be used as drums (pots, pans, boxes, etc.), and pretend to be "little drummer" boys and girls. Have fun singing and playing together.
- **Grandparent/Additional Gift Option:** Purchase children's drums or a children's musical instrument set

LAMB

- **Gift:** Lamb
- **Music:** "It Came Upon the Midnight Clear"
- **Story:** "The Little Lambs," Bob Hartman (recording available on iTunes)
- **Challenge/Activity:** Tell the story of Christ's birth
- **Grandparent/Additional Gift Option:** Nativity finger puppets to use to tell the story of Christ's birth.

BABY JESUS

- **Gifts:** Baby Jesus figure
- **Music:** "O Come All Ye Faithful"
- **Read:** Luke 2:1-20 and Matthew 2:1-12
- **Challenge/Activity:** Plan a "musical evening." Perform the Christmas carols you have learned this December, along with other family favorites. Invite your extended family or friends to join your family and perform their musical talents. Enjoy the music of Christmas. If you made pipe chimes, give everyone a chance to participate by playing a chime to accompany some of the Christmas carols.

INTERFAITH CHRISTIAN VERSION

This version could be used for anyone desiring universal Christian references. Useful for non-LDS families and others who may be sensitive to using LDS materials and music. All musical suggestions are classic Christmas carols. All books, stories, and challenges/activities are unique to this version. Add or substitute LDS resources, if you prefer, when using this as an additional Nativity-centered year.

ANGEL

- **Gift:** Angel
- **Music:** "Hark! The Herald Angels Sing"
- **Book:** *The Sparkle Box*, Jill Hardie
- **Challenge/Activity:** Open your "sparkle box," assemble it, and decide on at least one thing you want to do as a family to help others. Fill your box with blank pieces of paper, so each family member can write down the other "Christ-like deeds" they will complete this December. Make plans to open your "sparkle box" on Christmas Day, so everyone can share his or her experiences.

MARY

- **Gift:** Mary
- **Music:** "Silent Night"
- **Story:** "A Gift of the Heart," Norman Vincent Peale
- **Challenge/Activity:** Collect and donate some baby clothes to someone in need or some agency that distributes clothes to newborns.
- **Grandparent/Additional Gift Option:** A newborn outfit that your grandchildren can donate

JOSEPH

- **Gift:** Joseph
- **Music:** "It Came Upon a Midnight Clear"
- **Challenge/Activity:** Make popcorn, and watch one of your dad's favorite Christmas movies together.
- **Grandparent/Additional Gift Option:** Christmas DVD and dad's favorite popcorn

DONKEY

- **Gift:** Donkey
- **Music:** "Away in a Manger"
- **Book:** *Room for a Little One: A Christmas Tale*, Martin Waddell
- **Challenge/Activity**: Pretend to be the donkey that Joseph and Mary took to Bethlehem. Take turns being the donkey, Mary, and Joseph.

LAMB

- **Gift:** Lamb
- **Music:** "Oh Little Town of Bethlehem"
- **Book:** *Angela and the Baby Jesus*, Frank McCourt
- **Challenge/Activity**: Make dinner for someone who could be helped by this act of service.
- **Grandparent/Additional Gift Option:** Christmas aprons that you have made or purchased for your grandchildren to wear while they make dinner or when they do other Christmas baking

SHEPHERD

- **Gifts:** Shepherd, candy canes
- **Music:** "Oh Come All Ye Faithful"
- **Book:** *The Candymaker's Gift*, David and Helen Haidle
- **Challenge/Activity:** Open candy canes, and as you eat them, discuss what a candy cane represents.
- **Grandparent/Additional Gift Option:** *A Christmas Manger, A Punch and Play Book*, by H.A. Rey, and have the children punch and fold this paper Nativity and tell the story of Jesus's birth.

FIRST WISE MAN

- **Gift:** Wise Man
- **Music:** "We Three Kings"
- **Book:** *Boxes for Katje*, Candace Fleming
- **Challenge/Activity:** As a family, make a plan to send a Christmas package to someone. It could be someone in the military, a missionary, or someone suffering because of a natural disaster, war, or other tumultuous events.
- **Grandparent/Additional Gift Option:** Items that could be included in a Christmas package or consider enclosing a prepaid USPS Priority Mail package

SECOND WISE MAN

- **Gift:** Wise Man
- **Music:** "With Wondering Awe"
- **Story:** *The Legend of the Poinsettia*, Tomie dePaola
- **Challenge/Activity**: Choose someone your family will give the poinsettia plant to, and deliver the plant to them, and spend some time with them celebrating Christ.
- **Grandparent/Additional Gift Option:** Purchase two poinsettia plants, one for your children/grandchildren and one for them to give away.

THIRD WISE MAN

- **Gift:** Wise Man
- **Music:** "Joy to the World"
- **Story:** "Nellie's Gift," Anonymous (Appendix)
- **Challenge/Activity:** As a family, collect as many coins as you can during the next week, and give your donation to a church, agency, etc.
- **Grandparent/Additional Gift Option:** Money jar with a beginning collection of coins.

CAMEL

- **Gift:** Camel
- **Music:** "Angels We Have Heard on High"
- **Book:** *Humphrey's First Christmas*, Carol Heyer
- **Challenge/Activity:** Play with a brother and/or sister, and make them laugh today.

BABY JESUS

- **Gift:** Baby Jesus from your Nativity set
- **Music:** "What Child Is This?"
- **Book:** *The First Christmas, The King James Version*, Jan Pienkowski (illustrated book of Luke 2: 1-20 and Matthew 2: 1-12)
- **Challenge/Activity:** Have each member of the family choose one thing to put in your family's "Christmas box." Choose something that will remind you of Christ all year (star, poem, or scripture, etc.).
- **Grandparent/Additional Gift Option:** A special "Christmas box" and your special item that reminds you of the Savior

LOW-COST VERSION

This variation works well for families when you want to limit money spent on this tradition or on shipping costs, or if you are doing it for another family. Most materials are available online at lds.org.

Other Suggestions: Instead of purchasing a Nativity set, use one you already have, or consider making your own Nativity set with cloth, paper, wood, etc. (patterns for many simple Nativity sets are available online)

STABLE

- **Music:** "Once within a Lowly Stable," #41, *Children's Songbook*, lds.org.
- **Story:** "Gloves for a Shepherd," Sara K., age twelve, December 2013, *The Friend*, lds. org.
- **Challenge/Activity:** Make you own Nativity stable using a box, cardboard, or cardstock.

MARY

- **Music:** "Mary's Lullaby," #44, *Children's Songbook*, lds.org
- **Watch:** "The Coat: A Story of Charity" A true story from the childhood of President Heber J. Grant. http://lds.org/video/christmas
- **Challenge/Activity:** Give away something that cannot be purchased, such as a smile, a hug, an invitation to play, or a kind deed.

JOSEPH

- **Music:** "When Joseph went to Bethlehem," #38, *Children's Songbook*, lds.org.
- **Story:** "The Missing Egg," George Sterling Spencer, *The Friend*, December 2009, lds.org.
- **Challenge/Activity:** Do as many kind deeds for Dad today as you have time and energy to do.

ANGEL

- **Music:** "Oh, Hush Thee My Baby," #48, *Children's Songbook*, lds.org.
- **Story:** "Christmas at the Hospital," Kathy Johnson Gale, *The Friend*, December 2012, lds.org.
- **Challenge/Activity:** Be an angel by doing something for one day to create more peace in your family.

SHEPHERDS

- **Music:** "Stars Were Gleaming," # 37, *Children's Songbook*, lds.org
- **Story:** "Christmas Eve Drop-off," Lisa Harvey, *The Friend*, December 2010, lds.org.
- **Challenge/Activity:** Think about what you could drop off for someone or some family. As a family, make a plan of what to give and when you will make this happen.

DONKEY

- **Music:** "When Joseph Went to Bethlehem," #38, *Children's Songbook*, lds.org.
- **Story:** "My Gift to Jesus," Rachel Lynn Bauer, *The Friend*, lds.org.
- **Challenge/Activity:** Between now and Christmas break, go out of your way to be inclusive to someone who is often excluded at school. Share your experience and feelings with your family.

WISE MEN

- **Music:** "Picture a Christmas," # 50, *Children's Songbook*, lds.org.
- **Story:** "A Christmas Prayer Answered," Peggy Schonken, *The Friend*, December 2012, lds.org.
- **Challenge/Activity:** Choose a family that needs a dinner or a treat. Work together to make your surprise, and take it to them. It's even more fun if you can give anonymously.

SHEEP

- **Music:** "There Was Starlight on the Hillside," # 40, *Children's Songbook*, lds.org.
- **Story:** "The Empty Box," Anonymous (Appendix)
- **Challenge/Activity:** Make simple drawing of sheep, and glue cotton balls onto the sheep's body. Find a place to display your pictures.

COW

- **Music:** "Away in a Manger," # 42 *Children's Songbook*, lds.org.
- **Story:** "The Lights of Christmas," Hilary M. Hendricks, *The Friend*, December 2011, lds.org.
- **Challenge/Activity:** Help someone decorate for Christmas. Consider a grandparent, great grandparent, or elderly person.

CAMEL

- **Music:** "The Nativity Song," #52, *Children's Songbook*, lds.org.
- **Story:** "Warming up to the Lindsays," Marjorie A. Havens, *The Friend*, December 2013, lds.org.
- **Challenge/Activity:** Have each member of the family choose a family member or friend that they have a harder time being nice to, and be extra kind to them. Set your own time limit for how long you will continue your gift to them and thus to Jesus.

BABY JESUS

- **Music:** "Sleep, Little Jesus," # 46, Children's *Songbook*, lds.org.
- **Story:** "When Jesus Was a Child," *The Friend*, December 2013, lds.org.
- **Challenge/Activity:** Christmas memory box—Have each family member choose one thing to put in your family's Christmas memory box. Choose something that will remind you of Christ all year (a small Nativity figure of an animal or person, picture, poem, etc.). You can make a Christmas memory box by covering the lid and the main part of a box separately with wrapping paper.

SIMPLIFIED VERSION FOR YOUNGER CHILDREN

Young children love repetition, so I have selected six books to be used twice each, but you could also use a different book for each day, look in the Reference section under "Books for Younger Children" for additional suggested books.

Choose a Nativity set suitable for a young child to handle and play with; numerous child-proof Nativity sets are available. All books suggested are board books. All music is from the *Children's Songbook CD of the Church of Jesus Christ of Latter-day Saints.*

STABLE

- **Gift:** Stable
- **Music:** Play or sing "The Nativity Song," *Children's Songbook CD*, disc #2, song 1
- **Book:** *Baby Jesus Is Born*, Val Chadwick Bagley

ANGEL

- **Gift:** Angel
- **Music:** "Stars Were Gleaming," disc #1, song 38
- **Book:** *The Story of Christmas*, Patricia A. Pingry

MARY

- **Gift:** Mary
- **Music:** "Mary's Lullaby," disc #1, song 45
- **Book:** *Silent Night*, A Pageant of Lights Book

JOSEPH

- **Gift:** Joseph
- **Music:** "When Joseph Went To Bethlehem," disc #1, song 39
- **Book:** *Christmas Star*, Barbara Shook Hazen

DONKEY

- **Gift:** Donkey
- **Music:** "Christmas Bells," disc #2, song 2
- **Book:** *Christmas in the Manger*, Nola Buck

FIRST WISE MAN

- **Gift:** Wise Man
- **Music:** "Picture a Christmas," disc #1, song 49
- **Book:** *Silent Night*, A Pageant of Lights Book

SECOND WISE MAN

- **Gift:** Wise Man
- **Music:** "Sleep, Little Jesus," disc #1, song 47
- **Book:** *The Story of Christmas*, Patricia A. Pingry

CAMEL

- **Gift:** Camel
- **Music:** "Once within a Lowly Stable," disc #1, song 43
- **Book:** *O Little Town of Bethlehem*, A Pageant of Lights Book

THIRD WISE MAN

- **Gift:** Wise Man
- **Music:** "Have a Very Merry Christmas," disc #1, song 50
- **Book:** *Christmas in the Manger*, Nola Buck

LAMB
- **Gift:** Lamb
- **Music:** "Who Is This Child?" disc #1, song 46
- **Book:** *O Little Town of Bethlehem*, A Pageant of Lights Book

COW
- **Gift:** Calf
- **Music:** "Away in a Manger," disc #1, song 44
- **Book:** *The Christmas Star*, Barbara Shook Hazen

BABY JESUS
- **Gift:** Baby Jesus figure
- **Music:** "Little Jesus," disc #1, song 40
- **Book:** *Baby Jesus Is Born*, Val Chadwick Bagley

PART TWO

Family-Centered Traditions

"The wonder and awe of Christmas is just a beginning. Christmas reminds us that the babe born in Bethlehem has given us purpose for living, and what happens next to us largely depends on how we embrace our Savior, Jesus Christ, and follow Him. Every day we invite His Spirit into our lives. We see light in others; we hear the joy of children's voices that bring hope and anticipation for the future. We look for reasons to gather, to include, to serve, and to lift, while we learn what it really means to know our Savior, Jesus Christ.

—ROSEMARY WIXOM

TEEN/YOUNG ADULT VERSION

This variation is geared for a teenage audience, with age-appropriate short stories. The challenges are designed to nudge a teenager out of his/her comfort zone and make them more aware of the needs of others.

Other Suggestions: Your teenager may be resistant to participate, but you may be surprised how a well-placed story by their bedside may counter their resistance.

THE LEAST OF THESE

- **Gift:** Decorations for a new tree or a string of lights
- **Story:** "A Surprise Visitor," Erin Parsons (Appendix)
- **Activity:** Pick a sad or deformed Christmas tree this year, and make it beautiful.
- **Challenge:** Think of someone in your sphere of influence who could grow and be beautiful again with some love, attention, or decoration. Think of something you could do to brighten his or her life; it could be as simple as a smile in the hall or saying hello.

I'M GETTING NOTHING FOR CHRISTMAS

- **Gift:** Empty gift bag or empty gift box
- **Story:** "The Christmas Scout," Anonymous (Appendix)
- **Challenge:** Look for a way, like the young Boy Scout, to do a "good turn" for someone today.

WHERE ARE YOU, CHRISTMAS?

- **Gift:** New Christmas Music, include a copy of *"Where Are You, Christmas?"*
- **Music:** *"Where Are You, Christmas?* Song co-written by James Horner, Will Jennings and Mariah Carey (We like the Piano Guys version available online)
- **Challenge:** Take a moment to think about how Christmas has changed for you, does it still carry the same excitement? If not, think about ways you could bring the excitement back and do something to bring back the joy of Christmas.

UNCONDITIONAL LOVE

- **Gift:** Small framed Quote from Isaiah:
  - "Surely he hath borne our grief, and carried our sorrows...He was wounded for our transgressions, he was bruised for our iniquities; the chastisement of our peace is upon him; and with his stripes we are healed."—Isaiah 53:4-5
- **Story:** "The Whipping," Anonymous (Appendix)

CHRISTMAS CAME FLYING BY

- **Gift:** Candy bars
- **Story:** "The Candy Bomber," Babzanne Park (lds.org)
- **Activity:** Throughout the day, pass out candy to people who surround you. Try to reach out to people you may have never spoken to or do not know.
- **Optional Gift/Books:**
  - *The Berlin Candy Bomber,* Gail S. Halverson
  - *Candy Bomber: The Story of the Berlin Airlift's "Chocolate Pilot,"* Michael O. Tunnell
  - *Christmas from Heaven: The True Story of the Candy Bomber,* Tom Brokaw, illustrated by Robert T. Barrett
  - DVD: *Home for the Holidays: Mormon Tabernacle Choir and the Orchestra at Temple Square.* 2013

THERE IS A WAY

- **Gift:** Christmas treats to share with friends
- **Story:** "An Exchange of Gifts," Diane Rayner (Appendix)
- **Activity:** Perform a small, anonymous act of kindness for a good friend.

THE GRINCH

- **Gift:** A small Grinch figure
- **Book:** *How The Grinch Stole Christmas*, Dr. Seuss
- **Challenge:** Take a moment to reflect on your attitude lately. Do you need to apologize to someone for being a "Grinch?" Amend your attitude, and apologize.
- **Optional Gift:** *How The Grinch Stole Christmas* (Book or movie)
- **Optional Additional Reading:** "Maybe Christmas Doesn't Come from a Store," Jeffrey R. Holland

TOGETHER

- **Gift:** A game or other activity the family could enjoy together
- **Story:** "To My Big Brother, Danny, Who I Love a Lot," Blaine and Brenton Yorgason (Appendix) or "Once-in-a-Lifetime Christmas," Will Wright (Can be printed from various internet sites)
- **Activity:** Enjoy some time with your family.

GRATEFUL RECEIVER

- **Gift:** Blank "thank you" note cards
- **Story:** "A Handmade Ornament," Stephanie L. Jensen (Appendix)
- **Optional Additional Reading:** "The Good and Grateful Receiver," Dieter F. Uchtodorf

ONE SOLITARY LIFE
- **Gift:** A framed picture of the Savior
- **Story:** "One Solitary Life," James Allan Francis (Can be printed from various internet sites)
- **Activity:** Find an opportunity to bear your testimony about the Savior.
- **Optional Gift:** A copy of "The Living Christ: The Testimony of the Apostles." (lds.org)

UNCONDITIONAL LOVE
- **Gift:** Hot chocolate mugs and hot chocolate mix to share
- **Story:** "Doll Brings Lesson on Christmas," Adrianna Cabello (Appendix)

THE SACRIFICE
- **Gift:** A small Christmas tree to decorate and keep in their own room
- **Book/Story:** *The Year of the Perfect Christmas*, Gloria Houston or the story "Hard Times," Janet Anderson Hurren, in the Book, *Classic Christmas*.
- **Challenge:** Take a moment, and think about all that your mom is doing or has done to make your Christmas special. Is there some way you could help her in those preparations?

THE MIRACLE OF CHRISTMAS
- **Story:** "A Gift for Louise," Pearl B. Mason (Appendix)
- **Challenge:** Look around your room. Is there something of value that you could give to someone who needs it? Consider books, games, clothes, etc.
- **Optional Gift:** A doll to give to someone in need

ADULT VERSION

This format is for adults or anyone interested in stories and talks with greater depth. Most of the activities or challenges revolve around service.

Other Suggestions: A wonderful secret present for a widowed or single person. Also, consider using the stories and talks as a preparation for yourself during the Christmas season. Print the quotes and scriptures to display or memorize.

OUR GREATEST JOY

"There is no greater joy nor greater reward than to make a fundamental difference in someone's life."

—SISTER MARY ROSE MCGEADY

- **Gift:** A small bag full of food and toiletries
- **Story:** "I Knew You Would Come," Elizabeth King English (Appendix)
- **Talk:** "Waiting on the Road to Damascus," Dieter F. Uchtdorf
- **Challenge/Activity:** Wrap up small food items and toiletries. Put them in your car, and when the Spirit directs, hand one of your items to someone in need.

IF YOU'RE MISSING BABY JESUS

Maybe at Christmas, we should ask ourselves, just as Pilot asked the multitude gathered two thousand years ago, "What shall we do with Jesus, who is called Christ?"

—MATTHEW 27: 22

- **Gift:** A small framed picture of Baby Jesus, such as, *For Unto Us a Child Is Born*, Simon Dewey
- **Story:** "If You're Missing Baby Jesus," Jean Gietzen (Available as a book or can be printed from various internet sites)
- **Talk:** "The Search for Jesus," Thomas S. Monson or "The Gifts of Christmas," Thomas S. Monson
- **Challenge/Activity:** Give a blanket away to someone in need. It could be a blanket you have made, one you are currently using, or a new one yet to be loved.

LEARNING FROM A CHILD

"Our hearts grow tender with childhood memories and love of kindred, and we are better throughout the year for having, in spirit, become a child again at Christmastime."

—LAURA INGALLS WILDER

- **Gift:** A small jar full of pennies
- **Story:** "Handful of Pennies," Ella Birdie Jamison, as told to Norma Favor (Appendix)
- **Talk:** "Think to Thank," Thomas S. Monson
- **Challenge/Activity:** Find a young child; it may be someone you know, but it can also be a small child you come across in the store, etc. whose day might be brightened by the gift of a few pennies. Wish them a Merry Christmas, and hand them a small amount of money.

THE TRUE GIFT—THE GIFT OF YOURSELF

"It is Christmas every time you let God love others through you...yes, it is Christmas every time you smile at your brother and offer him your hand."

—MOTHER TERESA

- **Gift:** A basket of apples
- **Story:** "The Legend of the Christmas Apple," Ruth Sawyer (Appendix)
- **Talk:** "The Gifts of Christmas," Thomas S. Monson

A GIFT FOR A STRANGER

"Who can add to Christmas? The perfect motive is that God so loved the world. The perfect gift is that He gave His only Son. The only requirement is to believe in Him. The reward of faith is that you shall have everlasting life."

—CORRIE TEN BOOM

- **Gift:** A bag full of toiletries and other small necessities that can be handed to someone in need
- **Story:** "A Gift for a Stranger," Donavene Jaycox (lds.org)
- **Challenge/Activity:** Go through your closet. Find articles of clothing that could be given to someone who could use them. Donate them to a local shelter.
- **Talk:** "Jesus the Christ, Our Prince of Peace," Russell M. Nelson

A PERFECT GIFT

"Blessed is the season which engages the whole world in a conspiracy of love."

—HAMILTON WRIGHT MABIE

- **Gift:** Bread or muffins to add to the warmth and comfort of the season
- **Story:** "A Christmas Prayer," Rian B. Anderson (Available as a book or can be printed from various internet sites)
- **Talk:** "The Perfect Gift," Henry B. Eyring
- **Challenge/Activity:** Choose a neighbor you could do a secret act of service for, and perform that service.

A MOTHER'S LOVE

"Love is what's in the room with you at Christmas if you stop opening presents and listen."

—BOBBY (AGE SEVEN)

- **Gift:** A Christmas journal to write special Christmas memories and experiences
- **Story:** "Boxes Full of Love," Hope M. Williams (Appendix)
- **Talk:** "A Christmas Dress for Ellen," Thomas S. Monson
- **Challenge/Activity:** Take this Christmas journal and begin writing about your experiences this Christmas, and continue to record your experiences each Christmas. Write about your good deeds and your feelings of gratitude and love for the Savior and others.
- **Optional Gift/Book:** *Christmas Dress for Ellen*, Thomas S. Monson, illustrated by Ben Sowards

SPECIAL COMFORT

"The giving of gifts is not something man invented. God started the giving spree when He gave a gift beyond words, the unspeakable gift of His Son."

—ROBERT FLATT

- **Gift:** The book *Angela and the Baby Jesus*, Frank McCourt
- **Read:** *Angela and the Baby Jesus*
- **Talk:** "Christmas Comfort," Jeffery R. Holland.

THAT STAR

"There is much we can learn from the Wise Men. Like them, we should study the scriptures and know the signs to watch for as we all prepare the earth for the Savior's Second Coming. Then, as we search and ponder the scriptures, we will more fully desire to seek the Lord every day of our lives and, as a gift to Him, give up our selfishness, pride, and rebelliousness. When personal revelation comes to alter the plans we have made, we can obey, having faith and trust that God knows what is best for us. And ultimately, through lives of true discipleship, we must fall down and worship the Savior in humility and love."

—PATRICK KEARON, "COME LET US ADORE HIM"

- **Gift:** A Star
- **Story:** "Bethann's Christmas Prayer," Marilyn Morgan Helleberg (Appendix)
- **Talk:** "Silent Night, Holy Night," Joseph B. Wirthlin
- **Challenge/Activity:** Decide on a true gift you can give to the Savior this year.

A GRATEFUL RECEIVER

"The wonder and awe of Christmas is just a beginning. Christmas reminds us that the babe born in Bethlehem has given us purpose for living, and what happens next to us largely depends on how we embrace our Savior, Jesus Christ, and follow Him. Every day we invite His Spirit into our lives. We see light in others; we hear the joy of children's voices that bring hope and anticipation for the future. We look for reasons to gather, to include, to serve, and to lift, while we learn what it really means to know our Savior, Jesus Christ."

—ROSEMARY WIXOM, "WHAT HAPPENED NEXT?"

- **Gift:** A small bracelet or other small gift
- **Story:** "Angels, Once in a While," Barb Irwin (Appendix)
- **Talk:** "The Good and Grateful Receiver," Dieter F. Uchtdorf

THE BEST GIFT OF ALL

"Let us remember that the Christmas heart is a giving heart, a wide open heart that thinks of others first. The birth of the baby stands as the most significant event in all history, because it has meant the pouring into a sick world the healing medicine of love which has transformed all manner of hearts for almost two thousand years."

—GEORGE MATTHEW ADAMS

- **Gift:** The book, *The Scallop Christmas*, Jane Freeberg
- **Talk:** "What Shall I Do Then with Jesus Which Is Called Christ?" Gordon B. Hinckley
- **Challenge/Activity:** Express to your father or to any male influence in your life, how grateful you are for the sacrifices that he has made for you.

THE GIFT THAT CAN ONLY BE GIVEN BY YOU

"At the focal point of all human history, a point illuminated by a new star in the heavens revealed for just such a purpose, probably no other mortal watched--- none but a poor young carpenter, a beautiful virgin mother, and silent stabled animals who had not the power to utter the sacredness they had seen.

Shepherds would soon arrive and later, wise men from the East. Later yet the memory of that night would bring Santa Claus and Frosty and Rudolph---and all would be welcome. But first and forever there was just a little family, without toys or trees or tinsel. With a baby---that's how Christmas began."

—JEFFREY R. HOLLAND, "MAYBE CHRISTMAS DOESN'T
COME FROM A STORE"

- **Gift:** A gallon of milk
- **Story:** "Christmas Day in The Morning," Pearl S. Buck (Available as a book or can be printed from various internet sites)
- **Talk**: "The Light of Thy Childhood Again," Boyd. K. Packer
- **Optional Gift Book:** *Christmas Day in The Morning,* Pearl Buck

PERSONAL FAMILY STORIES/CREATE YOUR OWN

In this version, we are sharing some of our personal favorite stories written by family members, many based on actual events. Children love to hear stories about their parents, grandparents, or other extended family members. We are sharing our stories with the hope that you will share your own family stories with your children or grandchildren. We have included our stories in the Appendix if you would like to use them.

Look for stories in family histories, missionary letters, as well as asking family members to write or share their stories. Also, consider recording the stories in audio or visual format. One of our children's most cherished Christmas traditions is listening to Grandpa read the story of the first Christmas.

AWAY IN A MANGER: A MISSIONARY CHRISTMAS

- **Read:** "Away in a Manger: A Missionary Christmas," P. David Sonntag (Appendix)
- **Gift:** Santa hats
- **Challenge/Activity:** Go caroling as a family or, if you prefer, spend time together singing the songs of Christmas.

CHRISTMAS SPIRIT

- **Read:** "Christmas Spirit," Stephanie L. Jensen (Appendix)
- **Gift:** Some kind of teddy bear treat for them to enjoy after they hear the story
- **Challenge/Activity:** Have each family give something of theirs away. Talk about how each person felt when they were focused on giving instead of receiving.

GIVING A TRUE GIFT

- **Read:** "The Gift of a Lighted Tree," Alison R. Dunn (Appendix)
- **Gift:** Christmas lights
- **Challenge/Activity:** As a family, use the Christmas lights to decorate someone's home for Christmas.

A PARENT'S SACRIFICE

- **Read:** "The Red Bike," Stephanie L. Jensen (Appendix)
- **Gift:** Cinnamon Santa candy
- **Challenge/Activity:** Spend time together as a family looking at family photos and sharing family memories.

A FRIEND

- **Read:** "A Friend," Ruthie Dunn, as told by her mother (Appendix)
- **Gift:** A small bag full of treats for each person to give away
- **Challenge/Activity:** Like Ruthie, make a list of those people you know and those you associate with, and pray about that list. Find someone on that list who just won't leave your mind, and do something nice for them. Call them, drop something by anonymously, send a present, or invite them to join in your Christmas celebrations.

CHRISTMAS LIGHT

- **Read:** "Rudolph's Light," Stephanie L. Jensen (Appendix)
- **Gift:** A small red light or flashlight to remind them of how Rudolph's nose became red
- **Challenge/Activity:** Tell the story of Jesus's birth, using a Nativity finger puppet set or a Nativity set.

CHRISTMAS ON THE ROAD
- **Read:** "Christmas in the Mojave," Paul L. Sonntag (Appendix)
- **Gift:** Christmas music or a Christmas story on CD to listen to in the car
- **Challenge/Activity:** Write a note of thanks to your parents, thanking them for their Christmas sacrifices.

A HANDMADE CHRISTMAS
- **Read:** "Alvin's Christmas," Stephanie L. Jensen (Appendix)
- **Gift:** Oranges and peppermint sticks
- **Challenge/Activity:** Have each person think of a gift he or she could make for someone in the family. Make a plan, so each gift will be finished before Christmas.

A CHRISTMAS LESSON
- **Read:** "A Christmas Snow Globe," Alison R. Dunn (Appendix)
- **Gift:** A snow globe
- **Challenge/Activity:** Arrange to do a sub-for-Santa for someone. Ponder thoughtfully who you could help or which agency your family would like to use to help a family.
  - As a family, discuss memories of times you have truly felt the Spirit of Christ in your gift giving.

TWO CHRISTMAS PHONE CALLS
- **Read:** "Two Christmas Phone Calls," Darrell B. Sonntag (Appendix)
- **Gift:** Blank Christmas cards and stickers, markers, and pens
- **Challenge/Activity:** Write a letter to a missionary or someone who is spending Christmas away from home.

WISE MEN

- **Read:** "Wise Men," Stephanie L. Jensen (Appendix)
- **Gift:** Nativity sticker books
- **Challenge/Activity:** Spend time together placing the stickers in your sticker books. Talk about what it might have been like to have actually been able to visit Baby Jesus.

A GRANDFATHER'S TESTIMONY OF THE SAVIOR

- **Read:** "A Grandfather's Testimony," LaVon Jones (Appendix)
- **Gift:** Journals
- **Challenge/Activity:** Spend time together sharing your testimony of the Savior, or take time to write down and record your own testimony.

PART THREE

Christ-Centered Traditions

"*Born in a stable, cradled in a manger, He came forth from heaven to live on earth as mortal man and to establish the kingdom of God. During His earthly ministry, He taught men the higher law. His glorious gospel reshaped the thinking of the world. He blessed the sick. He caused the lame to walk, the blind to see, the deaf to hear. He even raised the dead to life. To us He has said, 'Come, follow me.' As we seek Christ, as we find Him, as we follow Him, we shall have the Christmas spirit, not for one fleeting day each year, but as a companion always. We shall learn to forget ourselves. We shall turn our thoughts to the greater benefit of others.*"

—THOMAS S. MONSON

STORIES OF THE SAVIOR'S LIFE

The focus of this format is to learn more about the Savior, His life, and His ministry. The hope is that families will learn and discuss the Savior's life together. For further reference, additional talks are given. Display a picture of each event from the LDS gospel art pictures or other available pictures. The Internet is a great resource for finding the quotes, nicely designed, and ready to be printed or ordered.

You may consider downloading and listening to the talks listed for each topic. Also, consider using: *The Life of Jesus Christ—Bible Videos*, lds.org.

Other Suggestions: For this year, decorate your home with the framed pictures of the events of Jesus's life. Wrap each framed picture, or use a single frame, and change the picture daily.

TEN LEPERS

Jesus went to a small town where he met ten men suffering from a disease called leprosy. They had faith in him and pleaded with Him to have mercy on them. Jesus told them to go and show themselves to the priests. On their way, they were healed, and their sores were gone, only one of the men turned back to thank Jesus.

- **Item/Gift:** Blank note cards
- **Scripture:** Luke 17:11-19
- **Talk:** "The Divine Gift of Gratitude," Thomas S. Monson

CALLING OF THE APOSTLES

Jesus entered Simon's boat on the Sea of Galilee and asked Simon to take Him out a little way from the land. Jesus sat in the boat and taught the people. When Jesus was finished teaching the people, He told Peter to take the boat to deeper water and let out their nets to catch fish. Peter told Jesus that they had fished all night and had caught nothing, but Peter said he would do as Jesus commanded. Many fish were caught by Peter and his brother Andrew, so many that their net began to break, so they beckoned to their fishing partners, James and John, to come in another boat to help them. The fishermen were very surprised to catch so many fish. Jesus then called Peter and Andrew to follow Him and become fishers of men. He also called James and John. They left their boats and nets and followed Jesus.

- **Item/Gift:** Swedish fish
- **Scripture:** Matthew 4:18-22; Mark 1:16-20; Luke 5:1-11
- **Talk:** "Followers of Christ," Elder Dallin H. Oaks

HEALING THE BLIND MAN

One Sabbath, Jesus saw a man who had been born blind. Jesus spat on the dirt and made clay, then put the clay on the blind man's eyes, and sent him to wash in the pool of Siloam. After doing as Jesus said, the man came away from the pool and was able to see. The man's neighbors were amazed, and he explained to them how Jesus had healed him. The Pharisees asked many questions about the healing and claimed that Jesus was a sinner for having healed someone on the Sabbath. When the man who had been blind was asked what he thought about Jesus, he said Jesus was a prophet. Later, when Jesus went looking for the man and revealed that He was the Son of God, the blind man fell down and worshiped him.

- **Item/Gift:** Sunglasses
- **Scripture:** John 9:1-17, 35-38
- **Talk:** "For I Was Blind, But Now I See," Thomas S. Monson or "Cameron's Picture," Ruth Cosby

CALMING THE STORM

As Jesus and His disciples were sailing across the Sea of Galilee, Jesus fell asleep. A storm arose, the wind blew, and the ship was covered with waves. The disciples, afraid they would die in the storm, awoke Jesus. He stood and told the winds and the sea to be still. The storm stopped, and the sea was calm.

- **Item/Gift:** Wind chimes
- **Scripture:** Matthew 8:23-27; Mark 4:36-41; Luke 8:22-25
- **Talk:** "A High Priest of Things to Come," Jeffery R. Holland

TEACHING IN THE TEMPLE

At twelve years of age, Jesus went with His family to Jerusalem for the Feast of the Passover. On the return trip to Nazareth, Mary and Joseph discovered that Jesus was not with any of their friends or relatives, as they had supposed. When they couldn't find him, they returned again to Jerusalem. After searching for three days, they found him teaching the learned men in the temple.

- **Item/Gift:** Chalk or a box of crayons
- **Scripture:** Luke 2:41-52; Joseph Smith Translation, Luke 2:46
- **Talk:** "Teach the Children," Thomas S. Monson

BLESSING JAIRUS'S DAUGHTER

Jairus, a leader in the local synagogue, asked Jesus to come to his house and heal his dying daughter. Along the way, Jesus was delayed. They soon learned that the little girl had died. Jesus told Jairus not to fear but to believe in Him. When Jesus entered the house, the mourners were crying. He told them the girl was not dead but sleeping. The mourners laughed, because they knew she was dead. Jesus took the girl by the hand and told her to arise. She arose from her bed.

- **Item/Gift:** Band-Aids
- **Scripture:** Matthew 9:18-19, 23-25; Mark 5:22-24, 35-43; Luke 8:41-42, 49-56
- **Talk:** "With Hand and Heart," Thomas S. Monson

RAISING LAZARUS FROM THE DEAD

Mary and Martha were devoted followers of Jesus. Upon hearing that Lazarus was very ill, Jesus traveled to their city. By the time He arrived, Lazarus had been dead for four days. Martha and Mary separately expressed to Jesus that if He had been there their brother would not have died. Jesus, showing great love for Lazarus, wept and then commanded that the stone be rolled away. Jesus prayed to Heavenly Father and commanded that Lazarus should arise. Lazarus arose and walked toward Jesus. This miracle helped many people to believe in Jesus.

- **Item/Gift:** A living plant
- **Scripture:** John 11:1-45
- **Talk:** "The Lord Has Not Forgotten You," Linda Reeves

MARY AND MARTHA

Mary and Martha both set about doing good. Martha was busy with preparations and serving the Savior. She complained to the Savior that Mary was not helping. Jesus explained that each was choosing a good part, and while Mary was sitting at His feet being taught, she was doing a "needful" thing, which would always remain with her.

- **Item/Gift:** A "to-do" list pad of paper
- **Scripture:** Luke 10:38-42
- **Talk:** "Choosing Charity: That Good Part," Bonnie D. Parkin

TRIUMPHAL ENTRY

Before the Feast of Passover, Jesus traveled with His disciples to Jerusalem. Two disciples were asked to go and bring a donkey. Jesus entered the city riding on the donkey. Large crowds of people gathered to praise and honor Jesus. Clothing and palm branches were spread in His path. The people rejoiced and shouted, "Hosanna; Blessed is he that cometh in the name of the Lord," (Mark 11:9).

- **Item/Gift:** Confetti or party blow horn
- **Scripture:** Matthew 21:1-11; Mark 11:1-11; Luke 19:29-38, John 12:12-15
- **Article:** "Reflections on the Saviors Last Week," Eric Huntsman

WOMAN TAKEN IN SIN

The Savior is brought before a woman accused of adultery. Jesus asks the crowd if there is anyone who has not sinned. If so, they can throw the first stone at her. The crowd slowly departs, and Jesus tells her that He does not condemn her, either. He forgives her.

- **Item/Gift:** A few stones
- **Scripture:** John 8:1-11
- **Talk:** "Mercy, the Divine Gift," Thomas S. Monson
- **Watch Mormon Messages:** "Lifting Burdens" or "Look to the Light"

CHRIST AND THE RICH YOUNG RULER

When a rich young ruler asks Jesus what he should do to gain eternal life, Jesus tells the man that he must keep the commandments. The young man tells Jesus that he has always been obedient to the laws of God. Jesus tells him there is one more thing he needs to do. Jesus tells the young man that he needs to sell all he has and give it to the poor. The young man heard what he needed to do in order to follow Jesus, but it was too hard for him to give away all his possessions, so he left Jesus's presence.

- **Item/Gift:** A small bag full of money
- **Scripture:** Matthew 19:16-24; Mark 10:17-25; Luke 18:18-25
- **Talk:** "The Straight and Narrow Way," Joseph B. Wirthlin

CHRIST AND THE SAMARITAN WOMAN

The Jews had no dealings with the Samaritans. Jesus, while traveling, meets a young Samaritan woman at a roadside well. He asks her for a drink, and she boldly questions him why He would ask a drink from a Samaritan. He teaches her that if she follows Him, she will never thirst. She then goes and convinces the people of Samaria to listen and learn from the Savior, and because of her testimony, many people came to believe in Jesus Christ.

- **Item/Gift:** Water
- **Scripture:** John 4:1-42
- **Talks:** "Give Me This Water That I Thirst Not: The Woman at the Well," Camille Fronk or "The Abundant Life," Joseph B. Wirthlin

THE LOAVES AND FISHES

A great many people are following Jesus, because they have heard how He heals the sick. When Jesus saw the multitude gathered, he had compassion on them and healed their sick. Upon hearing that there is no food for the multitudes who have gathered, Jesus takes five small loaves of bread and two fishes and blesses and breaks the food and gives it to His disciples to give to the multitude. All the people eat, and about five thousand people are fed.

- **Item/Gift:** Small loaf of bread
- **Scripture:** Matthew 14:13-21; Mark 6:34-44; Luke 9:12-17; John 6:5-14
- **Talk:** "Five Loaves and Two Fishes," James E. Faust

WASHING THE APOSTLES' FEET

Jesus, after eating the Last Supper, and knowing that He would soon depart from this world, pours water into a basin. He then washes the Apostles' feet and dries them with a towel. Jesus explains that He did this to teach them that they were to serve one another.

- **Item/Gift:** Soap or hand towel
- **Scripture:** John 13:4-15, Joseph Smith Translation, John 13:8
- **Talk:** "He Loved Them Until the End," Jeffery R. Holland

GETHSEMANE

Jesus and His Apostles go to the Garden of Gethsemane. Jesus separates himself from the Apostles and goes off to pray. Jesus repeatedly asks the Apostles to awake, and to wait and to pray for him. He asks the Father if this suffering might be removed from him, but tells Heavenly Father that He will do His will. He knew that the time had come for Him to suffer for the sins of the world. Enduring much pain and agony, He sweats great drops of blood as He atoned for our sins.

- **Item/Gift:** Olives or olive oil
- **Scripture**: Matthew 26:36-45; Mark 14:32-41; Luke 22:40-46; John 18:1
- **Talk**: "None Were with Him," Jeffery R. Holland
- **Watch Mormon Messages:** "None Were with Him"

CRUCIFIXION

At a place called Calvary, Roman soldiers took Jesus to be crucified. They nailed His hands and feet to a cross and raised it between two men who were considered thieves. Jesus suffered pain, thirst, and ridicule. When Jesus saw that His mother, Mary, had come to Calvary, He asked the Apostle John to care for her. As Jesus continued to suffer, He cried out to Heavenly Father, asking why the Father had forsaken Him. This great anguish was part of the Savior's suffering to pay for our sins.

- **Item/Gift:** The quote "Because Jesus walked such a long, lonely path utterly alone, we do not have to..." Jeffery R. Holland.
- **Scripture:** Matthew 27:33-50; Mark 15:22-37; Luke 23:32-46
- **Talk:** "None Were with Him," Jeffery R. Holland or "Overcome...Even As I Also Overcome," Neil A. Maxwell.
- **Watch Mormon Messages:** "None Were with Him"

EMPTY TOMB

After Jesus was crucified, His disciples laid His body in a tomb. A large stone was rolled in front of the opening. Guards were ordered to stand at the tomb to prevent His followers from taking His body. On the third day after Jesus died, Mary Magdalene and several other women went to the tomb to anoint His body. They found that the stone had been rolled away, and Jesus's body was gone. A young man clothed in white told them that Jesus had risen. Mary Magdalene ran to tell Peter and John that Jesus's body had been taken away. They went back to the tomb with her and found it empty, except for Jesus's burial clothes.

- **Item/Gift:** An empty box
- **Scripture:** Matthew 27:57-66; 28:1-8; John 19:38-42
- **Talk:** "He Is Risen," Thomas S. Monson
- **Watch Mormon Messages:** "He Lives: Testimonies of Jesus Christ" or "He Is Risen"

WALKING ON THE WATER

Jesus commanded the disciples to go before him to the other side of the Sea of Galilee. After a time, Jesus saw His disciples struggling with their ship in the storm. Jesus began walking on the water toward the ship. The disciples were frightened when they saw a man walking toward them on the water. Jesus called to them and calmed their fears by identifying Himself. Peter asked Jesus if he could come to Him on the water. Peter began to walk on the water to Jesus, but when he saw the strong winds, he began to be afraid and began to sink. Jesus immediately stretched forth his hand and caught Peter. When they were back in the ship, the storm ceased, and the disciples knew that Jesus was The Son of God.

- **Item/Gift:** A bottle of water
- **Scripture:** Matthew 14:22-33; Mark 6:45-51
- **Talk:** "The Beacon In The Harbor Of Peace," Howard W. Hunter

HIS RESURRECTION

After Jesus Christ died, His body was laid in a tomb, with guards posted to watch over it. An angel came and rolled back the stone from the opening. The guards were frightened and fell to the ground. Mary Magdalene and Mary, the mother of Jesus, came to the tomb. The angel greeted them, told them that Christ had risen as He promised He would, and invited them to look in the empty tomb. The women were filled with joy and went to tell Jesus's disciples.

- **Item/Gift:** A heart
- **Scripture:** Luke 24:36-43; John 20:19-20, 24; Matthew 28:16-20; Mark 16:14-20; John 3:16, 8:12, 11:25; 14:6; 1 Corinthians 15:20–22
- **Talk:** "Sunday Will Come," Joseph B. Wirthlin
- **Watch Mormon Messages:** "Sunday Will Come"

CHRIST IN AMERICA

After Jesus was resurrected, He came to the Nephites in the Americas. He invited them to feel the prints of the nails in His hands and feet, so they could know He was the promised Savior. He taught the gospel to the Nephites, administered the sacrament, healed the sick, prayed with the people, and blessed the children. Before leaving, Jesus blessed the disciples.

- **Item/Gift:** American flag
- **Scripture:** 3 Nephi 11-27; 3 Nephi 28:12
- **Talk:** "The Savior's Visit to America," Ezra Taft Benson or "Christ in America," N. Eldon Tanner

BIRTH OF JESUS

Mary and Joseph traveled to Bethlehem to pay their taxes and be counted. The time was close that Jesus would be born. Because there was no place for them to stay at the inn, Jesus was born in a manger. A new star appeared in the sky, and wise men began to follow the star. Angels sent shepherds to witness the Savior's birth.

- **Item/Gift:** A light or star
- **Scripture:** Luke 2:1-16, Matthew 2:1-12
- **Talk:** "Because He Came," Thomas S. Monson
- **Watch Mormon Message:** "A Gift to the World"

WITNESSES OF THE SAVIOR'S BIRTH

The focus of this format is to learn more about the witnesses of the birth of the Savior. This version comes with only one challenge, that of memorizing "The Living Christ: The Testimony of the Apostles," during the month of December.

Use the new film clips and pictures from the Gospel Library. Talks are supplemental and can be used by parents to help lead the discussion points. Time, most likely, will not permit the reading of the talks as part of the family time.

Other Suggestions: For young children, the process of acting out, and thus internalizing, many of the stories can be invaluable.

SAMUEL THE LAMANITE:

"And behold, an angel of the Lord hath declared it unto me, and he did bring glad tidings to my soul. And behold, I was sent unto you to declare it unto you also, that you might have glad tidings; but behold ye would not receive me." (Helaman 13:7)

- **Scripture:** Helaman chapters: 13-16
- **Talks:** "The Gifts of Christmas," Henry B. Eyring or "Converted Unto the Lord," David A. Bednar
- **Optional Activity:** Like President Eyring's family, act out the story of Samuel the Lamanite, with tinfoil balls being thrown instead of arrows. Remember, Samuel could not be hit.

JOHN THE BAPTIST

John the Baptist was sent to prepare the way for Jesus. He did so with conviction, courage, and faith. We learn from his humble example, unwavering testimony, and conviction about how to pattern our lives and prepare ourselves and our families for the Second Coming of the Savior. The importance of John the Baptist is summed up by the Savior in Matthew 11:11, "...Among them that are born of woman there hath not risen a greater than John the Baptist..."

- **Scripture:** Matthew 3: 11-17
- **Talks/Articles:** "John the Baptist: A Burning and a Shining Light," Robert Matthews or "Preparing the Way," Thomas S. Monson

ZACHARIAS

Are we like Zacharias? Do we need some time to remember the promises we have been given, so that we, too, can "open our mouths" and declare the wonders of God? Have we prepared ourselves for the return of the Savior? Where can we be found this Christmas season? What better gift could we give the Savior this Christmas than to keep ourselves worthy, to attend His holy temple, and prepare to meet Him when He comes again?

- **Scripture:** Luke 1:5-20, 59-79
- **Talks:** "Preparing the Way," Thomas S. Monson or "The Peace and Joy of Knowing the Savior Lives," Russell M. Nelson

ELISABETH

Have you ever stopped to consider the testimonies of Elisabeth and Mary, one old and one young, who both conceived under miraculous circumstances? What a blessing and support Elisabeth must have been for Mary, as they both began to prepare for the great events about to take place. And so, it can be said of both Mary and Elisabeth, "Blessed is she that believed: for there shall be a performance of those things, which were told her from the Lord." (Luke 1:45)

- **Scripture:** Luke 1:5-7, 39-45, 57-80
- **Talks:** "The Gifts of Christmas," Henry B. Eyring or "Twelve Witnesses of Christ's Birth," Joseph Fielding McConkie

MARY

Mary, the mother of Jesus, has been honored much, but it is evident that the Father must have chosen His most righteous woman to be the mother of the Son of God. To teach, love, and prepare Him for his wondrous ministry, Mary had a monumental calling. We can learn much from Mary and the simple testimony she bore, "Behold, the handmaid of the Lord; be it unto me according to thy word." (Luke 1:38)

- **Scripture:** Luke 1:27-38, 46-55
- **Talks/Articles:** "Mary, His Mother," Susan Easton Black, "The Peace and Joy of Knowing the Savior Lives," Russell M. Nelson or "Glad Tidings of Great Joy," Eric Huntsman

JOSEPH

Not much is known about Joseph, but we know that just as the Father chose a special and righteous woman to be the mother of Jesus, so Joseph, too, must have been specially chosen. What a responsibility Joseph was given to be the earthly Father of the Son of God.

- **Scripture:** Matthew 1:19-25 and Luke 2:4-5
- **Articles:** "Mary and Joseph," Susan Winters or "Mary and Joseph," Robert Matthews

SIMEON

What a wonderful example is evident in Simeon. Having been long promised that he would see the Savior before his death, the spirit directed him to the temple, so he could be there to give his prophetic testimony about the profound mission of the Savior. Can you imagine Simeon's joy and the spirit that he must have possessed to spend his whole life waiting to behold the Savior of the world? What effect did Simeon's testimony and blessing have on Mary and Joseph?

- **Scripture:** Luke 2:25-35
- **Talks/Articles:** "Christmas Comfort," Jeffery R. Holland or "Come, Let Us Adore Him," Patrick Kearon

ANNA

Like Simeon, Anna gave a prophetic witness, "to all them that looked for redemption" in the temple about the divinity of the Christ Child. But unlike Simeon, who was brought to the temple that day, Anna was not just visiting the temple that day, she was there all the time. From Anna, we learn that through regular attendance at the temple, we can be witnesses to miraculous events what will bring light into our lives and lift us from the "dark moments."

- **Scripture:** Luke 2:36-38
- **Talks/Articles:** "Witnesses of Christ," Dallin H. Oaks or "Come, Let Us Adore Him," Patrick Kearon

WISEMAN

"Where is he that is born King of the Jews? For we have seen his star in the east, and are come to worship him." (Matthew 2:2)

- **Scripture:** Matthew 2:1-2, 11-15
- **Talks:** "The Search for Jesus," Thomas S. Monson or "Of Curtains, Contentment, and Christmas," Dieter F. Uchtdoft

SHEPHERDS

We, like the shepherds, are invited to come and see. Are we going to allow excuses, pity, sorrow, or sin to keep us away from the Savior? Or are we going to make the journey with haste to find Christ, worship Him, and tell others about Him?

- **Scripture:** Luke 2:15-20
- **Talks/Articles:** "True Shepherds," Thomas S. Monson, "In Shepherd's Field," Annie Tintle, or "Come and See," Marvin J. Ashton

THE STARS IN THE HEAVENS

O Star of wonder

Star of night

Star with royal beauty bright

Westward leading,

Still proceeding

Guide us to thy Perfect Light.

"We Three Kings of Orient Are"

- **Scripture:** Matthew 2:2, 9-10 3 Nephi 1:19-21
- **Talks/Articles:** "The Star, the Savior, and Your Heart," Sue Clark, "I Found the Heart of Christmas," George Durrant, or "A Bright Shining Star," Thomas S. Monson

ANGELS

"And because he hath done this, my beloved brethren, have miracles ceased? Behold I say unto you, Nay; neither have angels ceased to minister unto the children of men...the office of their ministry is to call men unto repentance, and to fulfil and to do the work of the covenants of the Father, which he hath made unto the children of men, to prepare the way among the children of men, by declaring the word of Christ unto the chosen vessels of the Lord, that they may bear testimony of him." (Moroni 7:29 and 31)

- **Scripture:** Luke 1:26-38; Matthew 1:20-21; Luke 2: 8-14
- **Talks/Articles:** "The Ministry of Angels" Jeffery R. Holland or "A Season for Angels" Merrill J. Bateman

DAILY SCRIPTURE

This version provides a simple scripture reading for each day in December. Use this version alone, or combine it with other versions. We have provided each scripture for your ease in preparation. However, listed at the end, is a list with just the day and the reference.

DECEMBER 1   ALMA 7:10-12

"And behold, he shall be born of Mary, at Jerusalem, which is the land of our forefathers, she being a virgin, a precious and chosen vessel, who shall be overshadowed and conceive by the power of the Holy Ghost, and bring forth a son, yea, even the Son of God."

"And he shall go forth, suffering pains and afflictions and temptations of every kind; and this that the word might be fulfilled, which saith he will take upon him the pains and the sicknesses of his people."

"And he will take upon him death, that he may loose the bands of death, which bind his people; and he will take upon him their infirmities, that his bowels may be filled with mercy, according to the flesh, that he may know according to the flesh how to succor his people according to their infirmities."

DECEMBER 2   JOHN 1:3-4

"All things were made by him; and without him was not anything made that was made."

"In him was life; and the life was the light of men."

DECEMBER 3   2 NEPHI 2:6

"Wherefore, redemption cometh in and through the Holy Messiah; for he is full of grace and truth."

DECEMBER 4 **DOCTRINE AND COVENANTS 93:7-17**

"I saw his glory, that he was in the beginning, before the world was;"

"Therefore, in the beginning the Word was, for he was the Word, even the messenger of salvation—"

"The light and the Redeemer of the world; the Spirit of truth, who came into the world, because the world was made by him, and in him was the life of men and the light of men."

"The worlds were made by him; men were made by him; all things were made by him, and through him, and of him."

"And I, John, bear record that I beheld his glory, as the glory of the Only Begotten of the Father, full of grace and truth, even the Spirit of truth, which came and dwelt in the flesh, and dwelt among us."

"And I, John, saw that he received not of the fulness at the first, but received grace for grace;"

"And he received not of the fulness at first, but continued from grace to grace, until he received a fulness;"

"And thus he was called the Son of God, because he received not of the fulness at the first."

"And I, John, bear record, and lo, the heavens were opened, and the Holy Ghost descended upon him in the form of a dove, and sat upon him, and there came a voice out of heaven saying: This is my beloved Son."

"And I, John, bear record that he received a fulness of the glory of the Father;"

"And he received all power, both in heaven and on earth, and the glory of the Father was with him, for he dwelt in him."

DECEMBER 5   JOHN 3:16-17

"For God so loved the world, that he gave his only begotten Son, that whosoever believeth in him should not perish, but have everlasting life."

"For God sent not his Son into the world to condemn the world; but that the world through him might be saved."

DECEMBER 6   LUKE 1:46-55

"And Mary said, My soul doth magnify the Lord,"

"And my spirit hath rejoiced in God my Saviour."

"For he hath regarded the low estate of his handmaiden: for, behold, from henceforth all generations shall call me blessed."

"For he that is mighty hath done to me great things; and holy is his name."

"And his mercy is on them that fear him from generation to generation."

"He hath shewed strength with his arm; he hath scattered the proud in the imagination of their hearts."

"He hath put down the mighty from their seats, and exalted them of low degree."

"He hath filled the hungry with good things; and the rich he hath sent empty away."

"He hath holpen his servant Israel, in remembrance of his mercy;"

"As he spake to our fathers, to Abraham, and to his seed forever."

DECEMBER 7   MOSIAH 15:18-20

"And behold, I say unto you, this is not all. For O how beautiful upon the mountains are the feet of him that bringeth good tidings, that is the founder of peace, yea, even the Lord, who has redeemed his people; yea, him who has granted salvation unto his people;"

"For were it not for the redemption, which he hath made for his people, which was prepared from the foundation of the world, I say unto you, were it not for this, all mankind must have perished."

"But behold, the bands of death shall be broken, and the Son reigneth, and hath power over the dead; therefore, he bringeth to pass the resurrection of the dead."

DECEMBER 8   HELAMAN 14:4-7

"Therefore, there shall be one day and a night and a day, as if it were one day and there were no night; and this shall be unto you for a sign; for ye shall know of the rising of the sun and also of its setting; therefore they shall know of a surety that there shall be two days and a night; nevertheless the night shall not be darkened; and it shall be the night before he is born."

"And behold, there shall a new star arise, such an one as ye never have beheld; and this also shall be a sign unto you."

"And behold this is not all, there shall be many signs and wonders in heaven."

"And it shall come to pass that ye shall all be amazed, and wonder, insomuch that ye shall fall to the earth."

DECEMBER 9   ISAIAH 9:6-7

"For unto us a child is born, unto us a son is given: and the government shall be upon his shoulder: and his name shall be called Wonderful, Counsellor, The mighty God, The everlasting Father, The Prince of Peace."

"Of the increase of his government and peace there shall be no end, upon the throne of David, and upon his kingdom, to order it, and to establish it with judgment and with justice from henceforth even forever. The zeal of the Lord of hosts will perform this."

DECEMBER 10 MATTHEW 1:18-25

"Now the birth of Jesus Christ was on this wise: When as his mother Mary was espoused to Joseph, before they came together, she was found with child of the Holy Ghost."

"Then Joseph her husband, being a just man, and not willing to make her a publick example, was minded to put her away privily."

"But while he thought on these things, behold, the angel of the Lord appeared unto him in a dream, saying, Joseph, thou son of David, fear not to take unto thee Mary thy wife: for that, which is conceived in her is of the Holy Ghost."

"And she shall bring forth a son, and thou shalt call his name JESUS: for he shall save his people from their sins."

"Now all this was done, that it might be fulfilled, which was spoken of the Lord by the prophet, saying,"

"Behold, a virgin shall be with child, and shall bring forth a son, and they shall call his name Emmanuel, which being interpreted is, God with us."

"Then Joseph being raised from sleep did as the angel of the Lord had bidden him, and took unto him his wife:"

"And knew her not till she had brought forth her firstborn son: and he called his name JESUS."

DECEMBER 11   JAMES 1:17

"Every good gift and every perfect gift is from above, and cometh down from the Father of lights, with whom is no variableness, neither shadow of turning."

DECEMBER 12   ISAIAH 53:4-6

"Surely he hath borne our griefs, and carried our sorrows: yet we did esteem him stricken, smitten of God, and afflicted."

"But he was wounded for our transgressions, he was bruised for our iniquities: the chastisement of our peace was upon him; and with his stripes we are healed."

"All we like sheep have gone astray; we have turned everyone to his own way; and the Lord hath laid on him the iniquity of us all."

DECEMBER 13   LUKE 2:12-14

"And this shall be a sign unto you; Ye shall find the babe wrapped in swaddling clothes, lying in a manger."

"And suddenly there was with the angel a multitude of the heavenly host praising God, and saying,"

"Glory to God in the highest, and on earth peace, good will toward men."

DECEMBER 14   PHILIPPIANS 2:8-10

"And being found in fashion as a man, he humbled himself, and became obedient unto death, even the death of the cross."

"Wherefore God also hath highly exalted him, and given him a name, which is above every name:"

"That at the name of Jesus every knee should bow, of things in heaven, and things in earth, and things under the earth;"

"And that every tongue should confess that Jesus Christ is Lord, to the glory of God the Father."

DECEMBER 15   I NEPHI 19:9

"And the world, because of their iniquity, shall judge him to be a thing of naught; wherefore they scourge him, and he suffereth it; and they smite him, and he suffereth it."

"Yea, they spit upon him, and he suffereth it, because of his loving kindness and his long-suffering toward the children of men."

DECEMBER 16   JACOB 4:4-5

"For, for this intent have we written these things, that they may know that we knew of Christ, and we had a hope of his glory many hundred years before his coming; and not only we ourselves had a hope of his glory, but also all the holy prophets, which were before us."

"Behold, they believed in Christ and worshiped the Father in his name, and also we worship the Father in his name. And for this intent we keep the law of Moses, it pointing our souls to him; and for this cause it is sanctified unto us for righteousness, even as it was accounted unto Abraham in the wilderness to be obedient unto the commands of God in offering up his son Isaac, which is a similitude of God and his Only Begotten Son."

DECEMBER 17   MOSIAH 3:3-8

"And he said unto me: Awake, and hear the words, which I shall tell thee; for behold, I am come to declare unto you the glad tidings of great joy."

"For the Lord hath heard thy prayers, and hath judged of thy righteousness, and hath sent me to declare unto thee that thou mayest rejoice; and that thou mayest declare unto thy people, that they may also be filled with joy."

"For behold, the time cometh, and is not far distant, that with power, the Lord Omnipotent who reigneth, who was, and is from all eternity to all eternity, shall come down from heaven among the children of men, and shall dwell in a tabernacle of clay, and shall go forth among men, working mighty miracles, such as healing the sick, raising the dead, causing the lame to walk, the blind to receive their sight, and the deaf to hear, and curing all manner of diseases."

"And he shall cast out devils, or the evil spirits, which dwell in the hearts of the children of men."

"And lo, he shall suffer temptations, and pain of body, hunger, thirst, and fatigue, even more than man can suffer, except it be unto death; for behold, blood cometh from every pore, so great shall be his anguish for the wickedness and the abominations of his people."

"And he shall be called Jesus Christ, the Son of God, the Father of heaven and earth, the Creator of all things from the beginning; and his mother shall be called Mary."

DECEMBER 18   LUKE 2:1, 3-7

"And it came to pass in those days, that there went out a decree from Cæsar Augustus, that all the world should be taxed."

"And all went to be taxed, every one into his own city."

"And Joseph also went up from Galilee, out of the city of Nazareth, into Judæa, unto the city of David, which is called Bethlehem; (because he was of the house and lineage of David:)"

"To be taxed with Mary his espoused wife, being great with child."

"And so it was, that, while they were there, the days were accomplished that she should be delivered."

"And she brought forth her firstborn son, and wrapped him in swaddling clothes, and laid him in a manger; because there was no room for them in the inn."

DECEMBER 19   **LUKE 2:10-20**

"And the angel said unto them, Fear not: for, behold, I bring you good tidings of great joy, which shall be to all people."

"For unto you is born this day in the city of David a Saviour, which is Christ the Lord."

"And this shall be a sign unto you; Ye shall find the babe wrapped in swaddling clothes, lying in a manger."

"And suddenly there was with the angel a multitude of the heavenly host praising God, and saying,"

"Glory to God in the highest, and on earth peace, good will toward men."

"And it came to pass, as the angels were gone away from them into heaven, the shepherds said one to another, Let us now go even unto Bethlehem, and see this thing, which is come to pass, which the Lord hath made known unto us."

"And they came with haste, and found Mary, and Joseph, and the babe lying in a manger."

"And when they had seen it, they made known abroad the saying, which was told them concerning this child."

"And all they that heard it wondered at those things, which were told them by the shepherds."

"But Mary kept all these things, and pondered them in her heart."

"And the shepherds returned, glorifying and praising God for all the things that they had heard and seen, as it was told unto them."

DECEMBER 20 3 NEPHI 11:15

"And it came to pass that the multitude went forth, and thrust their hands into his side, and did feel the prints of the nails in his hands and in his feet; and this they did do, going forth one by one until they had all gone forth, and did see with their eyes and did feel with their hands, and did know of a surety and did bear record, that it was he, of whom it was written by the prophets, that should come."

DECEMBER 21 JOHN 14:27

"Peace I leave with you, my peace I give unto you: not as the world giveth, give I unto you. Let not your heart be troubled, neither let it be afraid."

DECEMBER 22 LUKE 2:11

"For unto you is born this day in the city of David a Saviour, which is Christ the Lord."

DECEMBER 23 3 NEPHI 1:13-14

"Lift up your head and be of good cheer; for behold, the time is at hand, and on this night shall the sign be given, and on the morrow come I into the world, to show unto the world that I will fulfil all that, which I have caused to be spoken by the mouth of my holy prophets."

"Behold, I come unto my own, to fulfil all things, which I have made known unto the children of men from the foundation of the world, and to do the will, both of the Father and of the Son—of the Father because of me, and of the Son because of my flesh. And behold, the time is at hand, and this night shall the sign be given."

DECEMBER 24   3 NEPHI 11:6-11

"And behold, the third time they did understand the voice which they heard; and it said unto them:"

"Behold my Beloved Son, in whom I am well pleased, in whom I have glorified my name—hear ye him."

"And it came to pass, as they understood they cast their eyes up again toward heaven; and behold, they saw a Man descending out of heaven; and he was clothed in a white robe; and he came down and stood in the midst of them; and the eyes of the whole multitude were turned upon him, and they durst not open their mouths, even one to another, and wist not what it meant, for they thought it was an angel that had appeared unto them."

"And it came to pass that he stretched forth his hand and spake unto the people, saying:"

"Behold, I am Jesus Christ, whom the prophets testified shall come into the world."

"And behold, I am the light and the life of the world; and I have drunk out of that bitter cup, which the Father hath given me, and have glorified the Father in taking upon me the sins of the world, in which I have suffered the will of the Father in all things from the beginning."

DECEMBER 25   2 CORINTHIANS 9:15

"Thanks be unto God for his unspeakable gift."

DAILY SCRIPTURE LIST

<u>DECEMBER 1</u>	ALMA 7:10-12
<u>DECEMBER 2</u>	JOHN 1:3-4
<u>DECEMBER 3</u>	2 NEPHI 2:6
<u>DECEMBER 4</u>	D&C 93:7-17
<u>DECEMBER 5</u>	JOHN 3:16-17
<u>DECEMBER 6</u>	LUKE 1:46-55
<u>DECEMBER 7</u>	MOSIAH 15:18-20
<u>DECEMBER 8</u>	HELAMAN 14:4-7
<u>DECEMBER 9</u>	ISAIAH 9:6-7
<u>DECEMBER 10</u>	MATTHEW 1:18-25
<u>DECEMBER 11</u>	JAMES 1:17
<u>DECEMBER 12</u>	ISAIAH 53:4-6
<u>DECEMBER 13</u>	LUKE 2:12-14
<u>DECEMBER 14</u>	PHILIPPIANS 2:8-10
<u>DECEMBER 15</u>	I NEPHI 19:9
<u>DECEMBER 16</u>	JACOB 4:4-5
<u>DECEMBER 17</u>	MOSIAH 3:3-8
<u>DECEMBER 18</u>	LUKE 2:1, 3-7
<u>DECEMBER 19</u>	LUKE 2:10-20
<u>DECEMBER 20</u>	3 NEPHI 11:15
<u>DECEMBER 21</u>	JOHN 14:27
<u>DECEMBER 22</u>	LUKE 2:11
<u>DECEMBER 23</u>	3 NEPHI 1:13-14
<u>DECEMBER 24</u>	3 NEPHI 11:6-11
<u>DECEMBER 25</u>	2 CORINTHIANS 9:15

DAILY QUOTE

This is a modified format; it consists of a simple quote for each day of December leading up to Christmas. This version is perfect to send each day via e-mail or letter to a busy member of your family. This is an excellent version for college students, missionaries, and those serving in the military.

Other Suggestions: Small Christmas goodies could be added as gifts.

COME AND SEE

"The shepherds were invited to come and see. They saw. They trembled. They testified. They rejoiced. They saw Him wrapped in swaddling clothes, lying in a manger, the Prince of Peace..."At this Christmas season I extend to you the gift of determination to come and see..." A young man in deep trouble and despair said to me recently, 'It's all right for others to have a merry Christmas, but not me. It's no use. It's too late.' ...We can stay away and complain. We can stay away and nurse our sorrows. We can stay away and pity ourselves. We can stay away and find fault. We can stay away and become bitter. Or we can come and see! We can come and see and know!"

—MARVIN J. ASHTON, "COME AND SEE"

A STABLE

"Once in our world, a stable had something in it that was bigger than our whole world."

—C.S. LEWIS, *THE LAST BATTLE*

HEARTS ARE SOFTENED

"What a glorious season is this time of Christmas. Hearts are softened. Voices are raised in worship. Kindness and mercy are re-enthroned as elements in our lives. There is an accelerated reaching out to those in distress. There is an aura of peace that comes into our homes. There is a measure of love that is not felt to the same extent at any other time of the year."

—GORDON B. HINCKLEY, "THE WONDROUS
AND TRUE STORY OF CHRISTMAS"

A CHILD AT CHRISTMAS

"Our hearts grow tender with childhood memories and love of kindred, and we are better throughout the year for having, in spirit, become a child again at Christmas-time."

—LAURA INGALLS WILDER, *A LITTLE HOUSE SAMPLER*

COME TO BETHLEHEM

"Come to Bethlehem and see
Christ Whose birth the angels sing;
Come, adore on bended knee,
Christ the Lord, the newborn King."

—"ANGELS WE HAVE HEARD ON HIGH,"
TRADITIONAL CAROL (THIRD VERSE)

THE GOOD AND GRATEFUL RECEIVER

"Every gift that is offered to us—especially a gift that comes from the heart—is an opportunity to build or strengthen a bond of love. When we are good and grateful receivers, we open a door to deepen our relationship with the giver of the gift. But when we fail to appreciate or even reject a gift, we not only hurt those who extend themselves to us, but in some way we harm ourselves as well.

The Savior taught that unless we "become as little children, [we] shall not enter ... the kingdom of heaven." (Matthew 18:3)

As we watch the excitement and wonder of children at this time of the year, perhaps we can remind ourselves to rediscover and reclaim a precious and glorious attribute of children—the ability to receive graciously and with gratitude."

—DIETER F. UCHTDORF, "THE GOOD AND GRATEFUL RECEIVER"

GOD BLESS US

"God bless us, everyone!"

—(TINY TIM) CHARLES DICKENS, *A CHRISTMAS CAROL*

NEVER CHRISTMAS, THINK OF THAT...

"Always winter and never Christmas;
think of that!"
"How awful!"

—C.S. LEWIS, *THE LION, THE WITCH, AND THE WARDROBE*

THAT STAR

"There is much we can learn from the Wise Men. Like them, we should study the scriptures and know the signs to watch for as we all prepare the earth for the Savior's Second Coming. Then, as we search and ponder the scriptures, we will more fully desire to seek the Lord every day of our lives and, as a gift to Him, give up our selfishness, pride, and rebelliousness. When personal revelation comes to alter the plans we have made, we can obey, having faith and trust that God knows what is best for us. And ultimately, through lives of true discipleship, we must fall down and worship the Savior in humility and love."

—PATRICK KEARON, "COME LET US ADORE HIM"

FELLOW PASSENGERS

"I have always thought of Christmas time, when it has come round, as a good time; a kind, forgiving, charitable time; the only time I know of, in the long calendar of the year, when men and women seem by one consent to open their shut-up hearts freely, and to think of people below them as if they really were fellow passengers to the grave, and not another race of creatures bound on other journeys."

—CHARLES DICKENS, *A CHRISTMAS CAROL*

A LITTLE EXTRA

"Christmas is doing a little something extra for someone."

—CHARLES SCHULZ

LET'S KEEP CHRISTMAS

"Would it not be well this Christmas to give first to the Lord, directly through obedience, sacrifice, and love, and then to give to him indirectly through gifts to friends and those in need as well as to our own? Should we do this, perhaps many of us would discover a new Christmas joy."

— JOHN A. WIDTSOE, "THE GIFTS OF CHRISTMAS"

REFLECTIONS ON THE LOSS OF HIS WIFE AND THE CIVIL WAR

"I heard the bells on Christmas Day

Their old, familiar carols play

And wild and sweet

The words repeat

Of peace on earth, good-will to men!"

—HENRY WADSWORTH LONGFELLOW, "I HEARD
THE BELLS ON CHRISTMAS DAY"

GIFTS TO LAY BEFORE THE SAVIOR

"Christmas and some of the cherished traditions of the season remind us that we, like the Wise Men of old, should seek the Christ and lay before Him the most precious of gifts: a broken heart and a contrite spirit. We should offer Him our love. We should give Him our willingness to take upon ourselves His name and walk in the path of discipleship. We should promise to remember Him always, to emulate His example, and to go about doing good. We cannot offer Him the gift of perfection in all things because this is a gift beyond our capacity to give—at least for now. The Lord does not expect that we commit to move mountains. But He does require that we bring as gifts our best efforts to move ourselves, one foot in front of the other, walking in the ways He has prepared and taught."

—DIETER F. UCHTDORF, "OF CURTAINS,
CONTENTMENT, AND CHRISTMAS"

READY TO KEEP CHRISTMAS

"Are you willing to stoop down and consider the needs and desires of little children; to remember the weaknesses and loneliness of people who are growing old; to stop asking how much your friends love you, and to ask yourself if you love them enough; to bear in mind the things that other people have to bear on their hearts; to trim your lamp so that it will give more light and less smoke, and to carry it in front so that your shadow will fall behind you; to make a grave for your ugly thoughts and a garden for your kindly feelings, with the gate open? Are you willing to do these things for a day? Then you are ready to keep Christmas!"

—HENRY VAN DYKE, *KEEPING CHRISTMAS*

LOVING OTHERS

"My idea of Christmas, whether old-fashioned or modern, is very simple: loving others. Come to think of it, why do we have to wait for Christmas to do that?"

—BOB HOPE

SEEK HIM, FIND HIM

"Born in a stable, cradled in a manger, He came forth from heaven to live on earth as mortal man and to establish the kingdom of God. During His earthly ministry, He taught men the higher law. His glorious gospel reshaped the thinking of the world. He blessed the sick. He caused the lame to walk, the blind to see, the deaf to hear. He even raised the dead to life. To us He has said, 'Come, follow me.' As we seek Christ, as we find Him, as we follow Him, we shall have the Christmas spirit, not for one fleeting day each year, but as a companion always. We shall learn to forget ourselves. We shall turn our thoughts to the greater benefit of others."

—THOMAS S. MONSON, "IN SEARCH OF THE CHRISTMAS SPIRIT"

HONOR CHRISTMAS ALL YEAR

"I will honor Christmas in my heart, and try to keep it all the year. I will live in the past, the present and the future. The spirits of all three shall strive within me. I will not shut out the lessons that they teach."

—CHARLES DICKENS, *A CHRISTMAS CAROL*

CHRIST'S PRECEPTS

"How many observe Christ's birthday! How few, His precepts!
O! 'tis easier to keep Holidays than Commandments."

—BENJAMIN FRANKLIN, *POOR RICHARD'S ALMANAC*

WHERE DO WE FIND CHRISTMAS?

"If you desire to find the true spirit of Christmas and partake of the sweetness of it, let me make this suggestion to you. During the hurry of the festive occasion of this Christmas season, find time to turn your heart to God. Perhaps in the quiet hours, and in a quiet place, and on your knees—alone or with loved ones—give thanks for the good things that have come to you, and ask that His Spirit might dwell in you as you earnestly strive to serve Him and keep His commandments."

—HOWARD W. HUNTER, "THE REAL CHRISTMAS"

GOD'S LOVE

"It is Christmas every time you let God love others through you...yes, it is Christmas every time you smile at your brother and offer him your hand."

—MOTHER TERESA

CHRIST CHILD

"For it is good to be children sometimes, and never better than at Christmas, when its mighty Founder was a child."

—CHARLES DICKENS, *A CHRISTMAS CAROL*

SILENT MEDITATION

"I wish for each of you a time, perhaps only an hour, spent in silent meditation and quiet reflection on the wonder and the majesty of this, the Son of God. Our joy at this season is because He came into the world. The peace that comes from Him, His infinite love which each of us may feel and an overwhelming sense of gratitude for that, which He freely gave us at so great a cost to Himself---these are of the true essence of Christmas."

—GORDON B. HINCKLEY, "THE WONDROUS AND TRUE STORY OF CHRISTMAS"

THE WONDEROUS GIFT GIVEN

"How silently, how silently
The wondrous gift is giv'n!
So God imparts to human hearts
The blessings of his heav'n.
No ear may hear his coming;
But in this world of sin,
Where meek souls will receive him, still
The dear Christ enters in."

—"O LITTLE TOWN OF BETHLEHEM," (THIRD VERSE)

WHO NEEDS CHRISTMAS?

"So who needs Christmas? We do! All of us! Because Christmas can bring us closer to the Savior, and he is the only source of lasting joy..." We need Christmas because it helps us to be better people, not only in December but in January, June, and November. *"Because we need Christmas we had better understand what it is and what it isn't. Gifts, holly, mistletoe, and red-nosed reindeer are fun as traditions, but they are not what Christmas is really all about. Christmas pertains to that glorious moment when the Son of our Father joined his divinity to our imperfect humanity."*

—HUGH W. PINNOCK, "WHO NEEDS CHRISTMAS"

RANDOM ACTS OF KINDNESS

In this format, you will do random acts of kindness each day in December. Use this list, or create your own ideas for random acts of kindness. Individually or as a family, review this list and choose a few random acts of kindness that you would like to do. Let the spirit guide you. As the season progresses, you will probably find that additional, unplanned opportunities to serve will arise.

✳ Return shopping carts for shoppers unloading their items into their car.

✳ Shovel snow for a neighbor or friend.

✳ Babysit for free for a young family that might need some time to go Christmas shopping.

✳ Buy a Christmas tree lot employee, Salvation Army volunteer, or someone who has a cold job, a hot chocolate.

✳ Offer a sincere thank you to a store employee, who may be feeling the stress of the Christmas season.

✳ Give a sincere compliment

✳ "Ding dong ditch" your neighbors with freshly baked goods or holiday trinkets.

✳ Deliver blankets to a homeless shelter.

✳ Leave a car wash pass on a dirty car.

✳ Leave a bottle of water for the UPS/FedEx driver with a note, wishing them Merry Christmas.

✳ Go to your local post office in mid-December, and pick one of the letters to Santa that they get every year. Buy and send or deliver the gift on Christmas.

✳ Leave an *extra* big tip.

✳ Feed parking meters.

✳ Host a Saturday-night party for the kids in your neighborhood. Eat popcorn and watch a movie or other activity.

✳ Hand out candy canes to kids in the store; ask parents first.

✳ Buy a gift card for groceries, and hand it out.

✳ Drop stuffed animals off at a children's hospital.

✳ Let someone cut in front of you in the grocery line.

✳ Pay a toll for the car behind you.

✳ Drop off doughnuts and a handwritten "thank you" note at a fire station.

✳ Make dinner for someone.

✳ Go caroling.

✳ Place notes wishing people a Merry Christmas on cars in the parking lot.

✳ Write a handwritten card, wishing a friend or family member a Merry Christmas.

✳ Gather clothes and shoes, and donate them to a shelter.

✳ Pass out gloves to those who could use them.

✳ Deliver wrapping paper and tape to a neighbor with kids.

✳ Buy a restaurant gift card, walk into the restaurant, and place it on the table of someone at the restaurant.

✳ Hand out balloons to kids shopping with their parents.

✳ Leave a bag of groceries on someone's doorstep.

✳ Open the phone book, pick someone anonymously, and send them something (movie tickets, book, a Christmas decoration, etc.).

✳ Leave a big note of thanks to your mail carrier or UPS driver.

✳ Leave quarters at a Laundromat.

✳ Deliver poinsettias to a local nursing home.

✳ Give a person who is working on Christmas Eve (i.e., a doctor, nurse, police officer, retail employee) something special.

✳ Pump someone's gasoline, so they don't have to get out in the cold.

✳ Take flowers to the hospital, and leave them for someone who hasn't had recent visitors.

✳ Hand out phone cards.

✳ Leave quarters by riding toys at the store.

✳ Leave candy canes under windshield wipers.

✳ Bring in your neighbors' trash cans.

✳ Take a picture for someone.

CHRIST-CENTERED TRADITIONS

✳ Simply smile, and greet an elderly person.

✳ Cheer someone on you don't know in a race or other sporting event.

✳ Donate blood.

✳ Write a thank-you note for someone who serves you.

✳ Buy or pack a meal for a homeless person.

✳ Donate new or used books to the library or school.

✳ Decorate the sidewalk with Christmas messages in chalk.

✳ Hand a passerby a goody bag and continue walking.

✳ Pass out turkeys to those in need.

✳ Call your mother just to tell her you love her.

✳ Hug your loved ones for no particular reason.

✳ Leave your favorite Christmas book in a public place with a note.

✳ Invite someone who is alone over for dinner.

✳ Introduce yourself to someone you always see around.

Appendix

Stories

The Littlest Camel

ANONYMOUS

Long ago in a far off country there lived a very little camel, and the littlest camel was curious about kings. This small camel wanted more than anything else to see a real king.

Kappe and Mogo, the large, large camels of his master, often told him about going to see kings, and about the large beautiful palaces, the kings lived in, and the stables where the cows were kept, how the hay tasted much sweeter and the straw was much softer in the stables of kings.

The littlest camel carried only everyday things to everyday people and he wanted so very much to carry wondrous gifts to a king. In fact, that was what he wanted more than anything else at all, to see a real king.

This night Kappe and Mogo were very tired and cross because they had just come from seeing a king—none other than King Herod. It had been a very long journey. They complained that the straw was poor and the hay didn't taste very good after the food they had been given in the stable in King Herod's palace.

While they were talking, their master and two other wise men came out and started loading great treasures on the large camels. They were to start at once on a long journey to Bethlehem with gifts for a very great King---the greatest king of all. The men pointed to a beautiful star in the heavens and said that it would guide them.

At last, all was ready to be loaded on the camels, but Kappe and Mogo were too tired. They could not carry everything and so the wise men decided the littlest camel would have to make the journey too. Goodness, how the littlest camel wanted to go. Now at last, he could see a real king. He could eat sweet hay, and sleep in the soft straw in a palace stable.

At last the gifts of gold, frankincense, and precious jewels were loaded on the camels' backs. The littlest camel heard his master say again as they started forth that the star would guide them.

The littlest camel liked stars very much—but he thought it rather foolish that a star could guide anyone. But the star shone brighter than ever and seemed to beckon them on. They traveled for a long, long time. The littlest camel was tired, oh, so very tired, but soon he would reach the palace and see the king.

But now the star had stopped. It shone down upon the stable of the every-day inn such as the littlest camel had seen many, many times at home. Only this one was in Bethlehem. How still everything seemed.

The little camel looked at the stable. He supposed the star knew how very tired he was and had stopped to let him rest awhile. Yes, that must be the reason. For surely this stable could never belong to a king. But the wise men were unloading their gifts and carrying them through the stable door. The littlest camel wondered where was the palace? Where was the king? This was only a very poor stable. The littlest camel tasted the hay—not so good—, and the straw was harsh beneath his feet. Perhaps Kappe and Mogo had been fooling him about all these things. But still the littlest camel wondered, why had the wise men gone into the stables? He'd take a peek. Quietly, carefully, he went forward and looked in the door. He saw no king. There were some shepherds as he had seen many times before. And then, one of the shepherds moved and the littlest camel saw a tiny baby wrapped in swaddling clothes lying in a manger.

There was a donkey, some wee lamas and a kindly looking cow, all watching the baby. The littlest camel looked at the baby too. Suddenly the littlest camel felt good and all glad inside. He wasn't tired anymore. He just felt good. The wise men were kneeling and placing their gifts at the feet of the beautiful baby. The littlest camel was so very happy. When he looked at the big camels, they seemed happier too, and more friendly. The hay seemed to become very sweet and the straw soft as thistle down.

Now for sure the littlest camel knew that he was looking at a great King. A king who would give peace and happiness to all the world, and suddenly he felt like kneeling down too, for he felt all worshipful inside. His legs were very stiff, but carefully he bent his knees until he was kneeling, and the large camels watching him bent their knees too. And ever since, camels remembered, and to this day, they still kneel just as the littlest camel knelt when he went to see a king.

Nellie's Gift

ANONYMOUS

The following story occurred in a Sabbath School meeting in Burlington, New Jersey. In a way it is a humorous story, but it teaches us a beautiful moral.

Did you ever want anything awful bad, then wake up and find it had come? Then you know how I felt when I received that package from my Auntie in New York and opened it and found a pair of real silk mits. Jack says they're just spenderific. Jack is my brother and he knows I'd wanted some ever so long, but I hadn't said much. Cause when you live in a little cuddled up house, and your father has to buy bread and shoes for so many.....Well, the money just flies, it does, before it gets around to what little girls want.

I don't know how Auntie found out about it unless Santa Claus told her and it wasn't near Christmas time neither. They were such pretty brown mits. Lilly Jones says, they're just the color of my hands, but I didn't mind for little hands will get brown when they have to weed the garden and do so many things. I look at them almost a hundred times in two days I guess--and then it was Sunday. Wasn't I glad?...I put them on and marched to church just so.

Jack says I held my paws like a sacred rabbit, but I never did see a rabbit with mits on.

It wasn't right to think too much what you wear when you go to church and by and by I didn't for we had such a good Sunday School I soon forgot everything else. A missionary man told us all about some poor little children away off. How a fire had burned down their school-house and they didn't have any nice homes r—clothes—r—nothing. But they were trying so hard to get along and to learn. And he said what was given to these little ones was just the same as giving to Jesus. Think of it---just the same as giving to the Christ Child.

Why I supposed everyone would give. Why SOME of those folks in that room was worth as much as ten or a hundred dollars. And yet that basket stayed mostly empty. I did wish I was rich, then at once I remembered about the poor Widow woman in the Bible. I'd read about it that very morning, how she had given her two mits, every living mit she had. It said so. So I took mine off and dropped them in the basket. And I was glad, even if my throat did all choked up. But they had no sooner taken the basket up, until the missionary man reached right in and took them out.

"Has any little girl dropped her gloves in the basket by mistake?"

Oh, how still that room was, I thought they were all looking all at me. And I just had to say something.

"It wasn't by mistake, I knew how the poor widow woman in the Bible gave her mits and so on..." And then those folks, just shouted (and laughed,) they did and I felt as I'd like to drop right down through the floor.

"If MITES doesn't spell mits, "(he laughed.)

Then the teacher put her arm around me and whispered, "Never mind, Nellie," and then she stood up and said, with her voice, all trembling, "Dear friends, this little girl has given her greatest treasure. Have we elder ones, done as much?"

Some how the money just poured into the basket after that. They brought my mits back to me, and the teacher said she'd show me how to earn some money to put in the basket. But, oh how full that basket was, an' when the missionary man counted it, his eyes grew all wet, and he said softly, although I didn't know what he meant, "And a little child shall lead them!"

The Empty Box
ANONYMOUS

Even though it was only September, the air was crisp and children were already whispering about Christmas plans and Santa Claus. It made the already long winter months until Christmas seem even longer. With each passing day the children became more anxious, waiting for the final school bell. Upon its ringing everyone would run for their coats and go home, everyone except David.

David was a small boy with messy brown hair and tattered clothes. I had often wondered what kind of home life David had and often asked myself what kind of mother could send her son to school dressed so inappropriately for the cold winter months, without a coat, boots, or gloves. But something made David special. It wasn't his intelligence or manners, for they were lacking just as his winter clothes were, but I can never recall looking at David and not seeing a smile. He was always willing to help and not a day passed that David didn't stay after school to straighten chairs and clean erasers. We never talked much, he would just simply smile and ask what else he could do, then thank me for letting him stay and slowly head for home.

Weeks passed and the excitement over the coming Christmas grew into restlessness until the last day of school before the holiday break. I can't recall a more anxious group of children as that final bell rang and they scattered out the door. I smiled in relief as the last of them hurried out the door. Turning around I saw David quietly standing by my desk.

"Aren't you anxious to get home David?" I asked.

"No," he replied quietly.

Ready to go home myself, I said, "Well, I think the chairs and erasers will wait, why don't you hurry home?"

"I have something for you," he said and pulled from behind his back a small box wrapped in old paper and tied with string. Handing it to me, he said anxiously, "Open it."

I took the box from him, thanked him and slowly unwrapped it. I lifted the lid and to my surprise saw nothing. I looked at David's smiling face and back into the empty box and said, "The box is nice David, but it's empty."

"Oh no it isn't," said David. "It's full of love. My mom told me before she died that love was something you couldn't see or touch unless you know it's there...can you see it?"

Tears filled my eyes as I looked at the proud dirty face that I had rarely given attention to. "Yes, David, I can see it," I replied. "Thank you."

David and I became good friends after that Christmas and I can say that with the passing years, I never again let the uncombed hair bother me, and never forgot the meaning behind the little empty box that sat on my desk.

Doll Brings Lesson on Christmas

ADRIANNA CABELLO

"Tell Santa what you'd like," Mother urges, as I stare suspiciously up at the whiskered old man. I eye him nervously. I don't want to talk to him, I don't even want to look at him, but I can't risk ruining my own Christmas. Like Ralphy and his Red Ryder, I am resolute. My Christmas will not be complete without a perfect, beautiful, porcelain doll.

I whisper my request and leap from his lap without waiting for the candy cane he is undoubtedly trying to hand me. I never liked those anyway. I cower behind my mom as I wait for my sister, Lauren, to take her chances with the scary old imposter. And that's when I hear it. Of course she asks for a porcelain doll. My eternal copycat.

As I stomp through the slushy mall parking lot I try to ignore her, but that proves to be impossible. When I try to hold Mom's hand, she grabs the other. When I fold my arms angrily in the car, Lauren does the same. Why couldn't I have been an only child? I try to ignore her for the next two weeks as I ready our room for the doll that is sure to be coming. From the corner of my eye I can see her, folding the blankets and polishing the tea set, just like me. Can't she do anything on her own?

When the glorious morning finally arrives we rush down the staircase to find that Santa did not disappoint. There, beneath the glittering lights of the Christmas tree, are two beautiful dolls. One with dark black hair for me, and the other adorned with bouncing blond curls like Lauren. My doll is perfect. Her bright brown eyes stare cheerfully up at me, set off by her rosy red cheeks. Her deep purple dress will match my bedroom perfectly. Surprisingly, I am so enthralled by my own perfect gift that I forget to be angry with Lauren, my copycat. We play together all morning and I even have fun with her, though I'd never admit it.

When it's time to go to Grandma's house, we buckle our dolls into their seat belts. I am literally counting the seconds until I get to show her. Grandmas are the best at being excited about Christmas things. When the minivan finally skids to a stop on the icy driveway, I throw the sliding door open. Grandma's going to see my doll first.

I sprint through the snow-covered grass, dashing up the stairs to the front door. Almost there. Right when my fingers touch the chilly brass knob, shattering glass echoes through the quiet evening air.

Whipping around, I see my sister, planted face first on the cold cement steps, with tiny shards from the little doll's face scattered in the snow around her. My voice catches in my throat, and I'm unsure what to say as I watch her eyes well with tears. I shouldn't care. I didn't want her to copy me in the first place. But against my will, all of my excited Christmas feelings are gone. I try to smile as I trudge into Grandma's house, but I can't seem to get over those little painted pieces lying in the snow.

Daddy carries Lauren inside, but she is inconsolable. She sobs on the couch and her crying makes me so upset I feel too guilty to even bother showing Grandma my doll. I hide it under my coat instead. It just doesn't feel right to be happy. I'd be destroyed if it were my doll that was broken.

Lauren is still crying when we get home much later that night. As Mommy tucks us into bed I stare through the darkness at the faceless doll that lies at her bedside. After what seems like hours, Lauren finally quiets down. I tiptoe across the carpet, snagging the doll by the hem of her dress, and sneak out of our bedroom to the stairs. At the bottom of the flight I heave a decisive breath. I know what I need to do.

In the quiet of the Christmas night, Daddy helps me pick the sleek black hair from my own doll's head, replacing it with the curly blond locks from Lauren's broken doll. When we've finished our work, even switching the dresses, the doll is barely distinguishable from its broken counterpart.

I place the new doll by Lauren's bed and crawl under my covers, excited for morning. Even though I no longer have my precious gift, I have something even better. This year for Christmas I learned what Christmas is really all about.

"Doll Brings Lesson on Christmas," Adrianna Cabello. *Deseret News*, December 22, 2010, Salt Lake City. © Deseret News Publishing Company, reprinted courtesy of Deseret News Publishing Company.

A Surprise Visitor

ERIN PARSONS

The day before Christmas, Daddy brought home two things: a skinny pine tree and an equally skinny black kid named Greg.

"Greg will be spending Christmas with us," announced Daddy.

"But Alan!" gasped Mother, "Christmas is tomorrow!"

"I know," replied our puzzled father, "that's why I told you today."

Mother threw on her coat and raced downtown, trying to guess what a displaced New York youth would want for Christmas. In the record shop: "The Screaming Meemies? The Asthmatic Six?"

Daddy was a psychologist then at Job Corps, a program to train underprivileged youth. He had often brought home stray students, but the others had at least been friendly. Tym, the oldest, took Greg upstairs to the guest room. Greg clutched his shabby bag to his short and slender frame, listening to Tym's questions but seldom answering.

The rest of us turned to Daddy. "Why for Christmas?" we moaned, "Why him?" Instead of answering, he told us a story. Greg had lived on the streets of New York since his parents threw him out at eight. He joined a gang, fighting with them and stealing food and clothing. Now 16, this was to be his first Christmas.

"He's uncomfortable around people he's had no experience with," Daddy explained, "but he's very aware of what's going on around him. Give him a chance, he'll respond." When Dad had finished, I felt a lump in my throat and a hard knot of guilt in my chest for not welcoming Greg immediately.

Our attention turned to the tree. Daddy had no trouble getting it through the door; it was paper-thin and had branches only on one side.

Daddy freely admitted that he had retrieved the pine after it fell off the back of a truck. "It'll be fine once we fluff it up," he confidently assured us. After 25 minutes of 'fluffing,' it was clear that the tree would take up no more than a fraction of living room space.

I didn't dare laugh at the awful tree to its face; I was afraid of offending its dignity. We waited in the kitchen, out of earshot, to moan about its sagging branches and how it listed to one side.

Greg permitted no pity; he had a certain, fierce pride. He was quiet, not taking part in much of the friendly banter, but listening carefully. I occasionally caught his smile as we struggled to decorate the disastrous Christmas tree. He patiently tied on branches, and it was Greg who devised a prop of bricks to make it stand straight. When we were finished, he eyed it thoughtfully. "It's an ugly tree," he said.

"Yes," I agreed.

He grinned suddenly. "I like it."

At dinner, Greg didn't join in as all six of us children seized serving bowls. As always, he wouldn't ask for anything.

Christmas morning, Greg opened his hastily bought presents with the rest of us. He seemed to like the Screaming Meemies and wolfed an impressive quantity of Christmas dinner, even by the standards of our voracious teenage appetites.

After dinner, Mother found him a warm ski jacket to cover his ragged coat, and Daddy located a spare set of skis. On the slopes, Greg caught on to the movements quickly, snowplowing contentedly and waving as we shot past on our way to the bottom. On the ski lift, I looked wistfully at the thick pines and spruces, covered with snow and dotting the mountainside.

"Why couldn't Daddy have brought home a pretty tree?" I complained.

Sister Tamara was more understanding. "Anyone can start with a fancy tree. Making one beautiful is better."

When we returned home, I examined our Christmas tree. Covered with popcorn strings and glass balls, it did seem a little taller and thicker.

At our Christmas program that night, Greg played a very credible Grinch in the play. The family was treated to another of his sudden grins as we applauded. And then Mother took out the Bible. She smoothed the worn cover. "Who'll read the Christmas story?"

Greg reached out a hand. "I will." He began, his soft voice hesitant at first, then gaining strength. His strange Eastern accent spun the familiar words into timeless beauty. We were all silent when Greg finished. As he shut the Bible, I glanced at our Christmas tree. The propping-up had worked; it stood tall and glittering in the corner.

Greg finished his training at Job Corps and moved out of Utah. In the years since, we have always gone to an expensive lot to pick out a thick spruce. But to me, none have ever measured up to Greg's first Christmas tree.

"A Surprise Visitor," Erin Parsons, *Christmas I Remember Best*, Salt Lake City, 1983, . © Deseret News Publishing Company, reprinted courtesy of Deseret News Publishing Company.

The Christmas Scout

ANONYMOUS

In spite of the fun and laughter, thirteen-year-old Frank Wilson was not happy. It was true he had received all the presents he wanted. And he enjoyed the traditional Christmas Eve reunions with relatives for the purpose of exchanging gifts and good wishes. But Frank was not happy, because this was his first Christmas without his brother, Steve, who during the year, had been killed by a reckless driver.

Frank missed his brother and the close companionship they had together. Frank said good-bye to his relatives and explained to his parents that he was leaving a little early to see a friend; and from there he could walk home. Since it was cold outside, Frank put on his new plaid jacket. It was his FAVORITE gift. He placed the other presents on his new sled. Then Frank headed out, hoping to find the patrol leader of his Boy Scout troop. Frank always felt understood by him. Though rich in wisdom, he lived in the Flats, the section of town where most of the poor lived, and his patrol leader did odd jobs to help support his family.

To Frank's disappointment, his friend was not at home. As Frank hiked down the street toward home, he caught glimpses of trees and decorations in many of the small houses. Then, through one front window, he glimpsed a shabby room with limp stockings hanging over an empty fireplace. A woman was seated nearby . . . weeping. The stockings reminded him of the way he and his brother had always hung theirs side by side. The next morning, they would be bursting with presents.

A sudden thought struck Frank: he had not done his 'good deed' for the day. Before the impulse passed, he knocked on the door.

"Yes?" the sad voice of the woman asked.

"May I come in?" asked Frank.

"You are very welcome," she said, seeing his sled full of gifts and assuming he was making a collection. "but I have no food or gifts for you. I have nothing for my own children."

"That's not why I am here," Frank replied. "Please choose whatever presents you would like for your children from the sled."

"Why, God bless you!" the amazed woman answered gratefully. She selected some candies, a game, the toy airplane, and a puzzle. When she took the Scout flashlight, Frank almost cried out. Finally, the stockings were full.

"Won't you tell me your name?" she asked, as Frank was leaving.

"Just call me the Christmas Scout," he replied.

The visit left Frank touched and with an unexpected flicker of joy in his heart. He understood that his sorrow was not the only sorrow in the world. Before he left the Flats, he had given away the remainder of his gifts. The plaid jacket had gone to a shivering boy.

Now Frank trudged homeward, cold and uneasy. How could he explain to his parents that he had given his presents away?

"Where are your presents, son?" asked his father as Frank entered the house.

Frank answered, "I gave them away."

"The airplane from Aunt Susan? Your coat from Grandma? Your flashlight? We thought you were happy with your gifts."

"I was very happy," the boy answered quietly.

"But Frank, how could you be so impulsive?" his mother asked. "How will we explain to relatives who spent so much time and gave so much love shopping for you?"

His father was firm. "You made your choice, Frank. We cannot afford any more presents."

With his brother gone and his family disappointed in him, Frank suddenly felt dreadfully alone. He had not expected a reward for his generosity, for he knew that a good deed always should be its own reward. It would be tarnished otherwise. So he did not want his gifts back; however he wondered if he would ever again truly recapture joy in his life. He thought he had this evening, but it had been fleeting. Frank thought of his brother, and sobbed himself to sleep.

The next morning, he came downstairs to find his parents listening to Christmas music on the radio. Then the announcer spoke. "Merry Christmas, everybody! The nicest Christmas story we have this morning comes from the Flats. A crippled boy down there has a new sled this morning, another youngster has a fine plaid jacket, and several families report that their children were made happy last night by gifts from a teenage boy who simply called himself "The Christmas Scout." No one could identify him, but the children of the Flats claim that the Christmas Scout was a personal representative of old Santa Claus himself."

Frank felt his father's arms go around his shoulders, and he saw his mother smiling through her tears. "Why didn't you tell us? We didn't understand. We are so proud of you, son."

The carols came over the air again filling the room with music. "Praises sing to God the King, and peace to men on Earth."

The Whipping

ANONYMOUS

Years ago there was a little one-room schoolhouse in the mountains of Virginia where the boys were so rough that no teacher had been able to handle them.

A young, inexperienced teacher applied, and the old director scanned him and asked: "Young fellow, do you know that you are asking for an awful beating? Every teacher that we have had here for years has had to take one."

"I will risk it," he replied.

The first day of school came, and the teacher appeared for duty. One big fellow named Tom whispered: "I won't need any help with this one. I can lick him myself."

The teacher said, "Good morning, boys, we have come to conduct school."

They yelled and made fun at the top of their voices. "Now, I want a good school, but I confess that I do not know how unless you help me. Suppose we have a few rules. You tell me, and I will write them on the blackboard."

"One fellow yelled, 'No stealing!' Another yelled, 'On time.' Finally, ten rules appeared on the blackboard.

"Now," said the teacher, "a law is not good unless there is a penalty attached. What shall we do with one who breaks the rules?"

"Beat him across the back ten times without his coat on," came the response from the class.

"That is pretty severe, boys. Are you sure that you are ready to stand by it?"

Another yelled, "I second the motion," and the teacher said, "All right, we will live by them! Class, come to order!"

In a day or so, 'Big Tom' found that his lunch had been stolen. The thief was located—a little hungry fellow, about ten years old.

"We have found the thief and he must be punished according to your rule—ten stripes across the back. Jim, come up here!" the teacher said.

The little fellow, trembling, came up slowly with a big coat fastened up to his neck and pleaded, "Teacher, you can lick me as hard as you like, but please, don't take my coat off!"

"Take your coat off," the teacher said. "You helped make the rules!"

"Oh, teacher, don't make me!" He began to unbutton, and what did the teacher see? The boy had no shirt on, and revealed a bony little crippled body.

"How can I whip this child?" he thought. "But I must, I must do something if I am to keep this school."

Everything was quiet as death.

"How come you aren't wearing a shirt, Jim?"

He replied, "My father died and my mother is very poor. I have only one shirt and she is washing it today, and I wore my brother's big coat to keep me warm."

The teacher, with rod in hand, hesitated. Just then 'Big Tom' jumped to his feet and said, "Teacher, if you don't object, I will take Jim's licking for him."

"Very well, there is a certain law that one can become a substitute for another. Are you all agreed?"

Off came Tom's coat, and after five strokes the rod broke! The teacher bowed his head in his hands and thought, 'How can I finish this awful task?'

Then he heard the class sobbing, and what did he see? Little Jim had reached up and caught Tom with both arms around his neck. "Tom, I'm sorry that I stole your lunch, but I was awful hungry. Tom, I will love you till I die for taking my licking for me! Yes, I will love you forever!"

An Exchange of Gifts

DIANE RAYNER

I grew up believing that Christmas was a time when wise and royal visitors came riding, when at midnight the barnyard animals talked to one another, and in the light of a fabulous star, God came down to us as a little child. Christmas to me has always been a time of enchantment, and never more so than the year that my son Marty was eight. That was the same year my three children and I had moved into a cozy new trailer home in a forested area just outside of Redmond, Washington. As the holiday approached, our spirits were light, not to be dampened even by the winter rains that swept down Puget Sound to douse our home and make our floors muddy.

Throughout that December, Marty had been the most spirited and busiest of us all. He was my youngest—a cheerful boy, blond haired and playful, with a quaint habit of looking up at you and cocking his head like a puppy when you talked to him. Actually, the reason for this was that Marty was deaf in his left ear, but it was a condition that he never complained about.

For weeks I'd been watching Marty. I knew something was going on with him that he was not telling me about. I saw how eagerly he made his bed, took out the trash, and carefully set the table and helped Rick and Pam prepare dinner before I got home from work. I saw how he silently collected his tiny allowance and tucked it away, spending not a cent of it. I had no idea what all this quiet activity was about, but I suspected that somehow it had something to do with Kenny. Kenny was Marty's friend, and ever since they'd found each other in the springtime, they were seldom apart. If you called to one, you got them both. Their world was in the meadow, a horse pasture broken by a small winding stream, where the boys caught frogs and snakes, where they'd search for arrowheads or hidden treasure, or where they'd spend an afternoon feeding peanuts to the squirrels.

110

Times were hard for our little family, and we had to do some scrimping to get by. But Kenny's family was desperately poor and his mother was having a real struggle feeding and clothing her two children.

How we worked as we did each year to make our home festive for the holiday! Our Christmas gifts were handcrafted and hidden away, and ornaments were strung about the place. Marty and Kenny would sometimes help; but then, in a flash, one would whisper to the other, and they would be out the door and into the horse pasture and sliding cautiously under the electric fence that separated our home from Kenny's.

One night shortly before Christmas—Marty came into the kitchen and told me in a tone mixed with great pleasure and pride, "Mom, I've bought Kenny a Christmas present. Want to see it?" So that's what he's been up to, I said to myself. It's something he's wanted for a long, long time, Mom," Marty said, and he pulled from his pocket a small box. Lifting the lid, I gazed at the pocket compass that my son had been saving all those allowances to buy. A little compass to point an eight-year-old adventurer through the woods.

"It's a lovely gift, Martin," I said, but even as I spoke, a disturbing thought came to mind. Kenny's family could barely afford to exchange gifts among themselves, and giving presents to others was out of the question. I was sure Kenny's proud mother would not permit her son to receive something he could not return in kind. Gently, carefully, I talked over the problem with Marty. He understood what I was saying. "I know, Mom, I know, but what if it was a secret? What if they never found out who gave it?"

I didn't know how to answer him. I just didn't know. And so the matter was left up in the air.

The day before Christmas was rainy, cold, and gray. The three kids and I all but fell over one another as we put finishing touches on Christmas secrets and prepared for family and friends who would be dropping by. Night settled in. The rain continued. I looked out the window over the sink and felt an odd sadness. How mundane the rain seemed for a Christmas Eve. Would wise men and kings come riding on such a night? I doubted it. It seemed to me that strange and wonderful things happened only on clear nights, nights when one could at least see a star in the heavens.

I turned from the window, and as I checked on the ham and homemade bread in the oven, I saw Marty slip out the door. He wore his coat over his pajamas. I knew he was

111

clutching a tiny, colorfully wrapped box in his pocket. Later he told me what happened to him that night. Down through the soggy pasture he'd gone, then a quick slide under the electric fence, and across the yard to Kenny's house. Up the steps on tiptoes, shoes squishing, opening the screen door just a crack, the gift placed on the doorstep, then a deep breath, a reach for the doorbell, and a press on it—hard. Quickly Marty turned, ran down the steps, and across the yard in a wild race to get away unnoticed. Then, suddenly, he banged into the electric fence. The shock sent him reeling. He lay stunned on the wet ground. His body tingled and he gasped for breath. Then slowly, weakly, confused, and frightened, he struggled back home.

"Marty," we cried as he stumbled through the door, "what happened?"

"I forgot about the fence, and it knocked me down." I hugged his muddy little body to me. He was still dazed, and there was a red mark from the fence beginning to blister on his face from his mouth to his ear. Quickly I treated the blister, and with a warm cup of cocoa soothing him, Marty's bright spirits returned. I tucked him into bed, and just before he fell asleep, he looked up at me and said, "Mom, I'm sure Kenny didn't see me."

That Christmas Eve, I went to bed unhappy and puzzled. The encounter with the electric fence seemed such a cruel thing to happen to a little boy while on the purest kind of Christmas mission, doing what the Lord wants us all to do, giving to others and giving in secret at that. I did not sleep well that night. Somewhere deep inside, I think I must have been feeling the disappointment that the night of Christmas had come, and it had been just an ordinary, problem-filled night—no mysterious enchantment at all.

But I was wrong. By morning, the rain had stopped, and the sun was shining. The streak on Marty's face was very red, but I could tell that the burn was not serious. We opened our presents, and soon, not unexpectedly, Kenny was knocking on the door, eager to show Marty his new compass and to tell about the mystery of its arrival. It was plain that Kenny didn't suspect Marty at all, and while the two of them talked, Marty just smiled and smiled. Then I noticed that while the two boys were comparing their Christmases, nodding and gesturing and chattering away, Marty was not cocking his head. When Kenny was talking, Marty was listening with his deaf ear—the ear that had slammed into the fence.

Weeks later, a report came from the school nurse verifying what Marty and I already knew: "Marty now has complete hearing in both ears." The mystery of how Marty regained his hearing, and still has it, remains just that—a mystery. Doctors suspect, of course, that the shock from the electric fence was somehow responsible. Perhaps so. Whatever the reason, I just remain thankful to God for the good exchange of gifts made that night.

So, you see, strange and wonderful things will happen on the night of our Lord's birth. And one does not have to have a clear night, either, to follow a fabulous star.

A Handmade Ornament

STEPHANIE L. JENSEN

Salty dough covered my hands while making the ornament for my ballet teacher, Ms. Sara. In school, we made ornaments. Everyone else was making trees and Santa Clauses, but I wanted to make ballet slippers for my teacher. She was a picture perfect ballerina with brown hair in a bun and a black leotard.

I could imagine the ornament hanging on her tree, the pink slippers up at the very top near the star. I'll admit, it got a little messy, and the paint job wasn't perfect. I had to make my own shape, but I thought it looked pretty good.

The day before Christmas Eve, I got out my ornament, wrapped it in tissue paper, and put it in a bag. I couldn't wait to give it to her.

At the end of the lesson, I got out my present. She was talking to the mom of another student in our class, so I patiently waited until she was done.

"Here, Ms. Sara," I said. "I have a present for you."

"Oh, thank you, Hannah," said Ms. Sara. She held the bag.

Ms. Sara opened the bag, gently unwrapping the tissue paper. She picked up the ornament.

"What is it?" Ms. Sara asked.

"It's a pair of ballet slippers," I said. "It's an ornament for your tree."

She held it up with two fingers, eyeing it like it was diseased. "Angie, will you get the next class started?" she said, taking the ornament. "Thank you, Hannah," she said, looking at me. "I'll see you in a couple of weeks." she said briskly and then walked away.

I went out to the car to meet my mom. "Hi, Hannah," my mom said. "How was ballet today?"

"Oh, I forgot my bag; I'll be right back!" I said. I ran back into the studio to pick up my bag, and there, sitting in the garbage, was my ornament. The one I had worked so hard on. I picked the ornament out of the garbage. I held the wrapped ornament and turned around. I walked quickly to the car and opened the door. I turned away from my mom with my ornament in my hand. I looked at the melting snow outside.

"Hannah, what's wrong?" Mom asked. "Did you forget to give Ms. Sara her present?"

"No, Mom," I said angrily. "She didn't want it."

"Of course she wanted it," Mom said. "She was just too busy to worry about a Christmas present."

"No, she didn't want it at all," I said crying even harder.

"Oh, Hannah," Mom said. "Let's take it home and put it on the very top branch of our tree."

Ms. Sara didn't want my ornament. I guess she didn't like handmade presents. I had spent a whole week working on it, and she tossed it aside as if it were sick with the flu. I felt devastated and angry at her for disregarding something that seemed to be a part of me. I took the ornament, not sure where to put it or what to do with it. I placed it under my pillow and cried.

Used by permission of the author.

To My Big Brother, Danny, Who I Love a Lot

BLAINE AND BRENT YORGASON

Even though it's been two years, I still get this guilty feeling around Christmastime. I just can't help thinking about my brother, Danny, and wishing I'd returned even half the love he shared with me.

Danny was born when I was four, and by the time I was six, I had picked up on enough adult conversation to know that my parents were concerned about his development. He was, indeed, partially retarded, but my mother continually referred to him as "special." From the beginning this bothered me; wasn't I special in some way? I began to suspect that I'd be forgotten, except as a guardian for my "special" brother. I decided to avoid that if at all possible.

I still remember the day I cleverly slipped away from his clinging attention about a block away from our house. I tricked him and left him crying on the sidewalk so I could play with my own friends. When I started home, I found him right where I'd left him, beaming at me in spite of his tear-stained eyes and runny nose. Thankfully, he hugged my arm and murmured my name all the way up the block. I fully expected to be in all kinds of trouble for my foul deed, but Danny never said a word about it to our parents. In fact, he came to my room that night to thank me for helping him when he was lost.

You'd think I'd learned from such an experience, but I didn't. I continued to tease him and to leave him out of my activities as much as possible. One time Danny showed up where my friends were, and I lead the group in calling him names.

Through my high school years, I avoided Danny almost entirely, having little to do with him even at home. It wasn't so much that I felt burdened to take care of him any more; I just hated to be connected with him, because it might affect my image. I was relieved when my acceptance to college came, because I knew that there I wouldn't have to worry about Danny's little feet clumsily pounding the pavement behind me.

Mom occasionally wrote to me, telling of how Danny would sometimes cry for hours concerning his big brother's absence. She mentioned that the only consolation for Danny was that his big brother was coming home for Christmas in two weeks.

Danny had been saving his money for over two years in order to buy a bike, which he had seen some time ago in a store window. This would be the Christmas that he would be able to afford the purchase of it with his own savings. Danny was now thirteen, and Mom had gotten him a paper route, which enabled him to save a little money.

Though she didn't tell me about it at the time, Mom knew about Danny's Christmas plans for me. First she found his piggy bank empty on the floor in his bedroom; then she saw the shopping bag from Hampstead's Camera Shop. It wasn't hard to figure out that Danny has been listening on the extension when Mom had phoned me to ask what I'd like for Christmas. Danny had sacrificed his bicycle to buy me the camera I'd mentioned to Mom.

At the end of the five-hour bus ride home, I was glad to be there. Walking from the bus station, I looked at the Christmas decorations on the houses and thought only what a comfort it would be to spend ten days lying around my own house. Certainly I didn't expect what I found when I walked in.

The rooms were dark, but I could hear Mom's voice, and I followed the sound to Danny's room. There, through the slightly open door, I saw my mother kneeling by Danny's bed, cradling him in her arms and rocking gently.

Dad came up and took my arm, gently steering me into the living room where he explained Danny's accident. It seemed that Danny had seen a boy fall through the thin ice on Sluice Pond. Leaving the newspapers he was delivering, Danny ran to the boy's aid, only to crash through the ice himself. By the time someone fished him out, Danny was unconscious and remained so for several hours. He'd developed pneumonia and some other complications.

Christmas Eve came, and Danny grew worse. That night, Mom told me Danny wished to see me. When I approached his bedside, he immediately clenched my arm with his hands. Mom, on cue, entered the room with a wrapped package and handed it to me. I read the card attached: "To my big brother who I love a lot. From Danny."

I opened the package, and Danny smiled. Then he asked if I had a present for him. I really hadn't, but I said I did. I said it was so big that I had to leave it at the bus station, and it would be delivered tomorrow.

I hurried quickly out of the room with tears in my eyes and hopes of catching the store open where Danny's long-awaited bicycle hung. What luck! The store was still open, and I made the purchase. I carried the bike home and placed it in front of the tree, attaching a small card: "To my little brother who I love a lot. From David."

All to no avail. Danny never saw his present from me. He never heard me say, "I love you." He died that night in his sleep.

Excerpt from Blaine M. Yorgason and Brenton G. Yorgason, *Others*, Salt Lake City, Bookcraft, 1978, 36. Permission granted by Blaine Yorgason.

A Gift for Louise

PEARL B. MASON

I was teaching fourth grade in my hometown in Wyoming. It was the day before our Christmas program was to be given. School routine was forgotten as we sang carols and rehearsed plays under the magic spell of the lighted Christmas tree. Names were drawn, and apparently all the pupils had brought their gifts.

In this class was a girl who was different from the rest of the pupils, because of her almost indescribably unkempt, frowsy appearance. She came from a family of nine healthy, robust, aggressive children. There was none of this in Louise. I never think of her but I picture a frail child standing before me in a long, loose dress, pinned at the neck with a big safety pin, and a sash wound around her waist trying to keep the oversized dress on her tiny frame. Her mouse hair always stood out like cocklebur and she would wait for me every morning at the top of the stairs and stammer, "G-g-good morning," to me. I always responded kindly to her greeting, and her face would light up with a smile that would almost turn her inside out. If Louise had any enthusiasm for anything, it was to find someone who would befriend her.

I had wondered who had drawn Louise's name. Since I heard nothing, I had supposed everyone had accepted the name he had drawn with kindness and all was well.

As I returned to my room after dismissing the class for the day, I was surprised to find one of the girls waiting beside my desk. She held a small square box in her hand, and quietly she began to tell me her story.

Walter, the most popular boy in the class, had drawn Louise's name and had wrapped a big piece of coal in tissue paper for her. It was easily recognizable under the tree. Hazel was afraid it would make Louise cry. Could she please replace it with this present? She had earned it by helping her father in his general store after school.

Well, the big moment finally arrived. The Christmas program was over and Santa had come in to distribute the presents. No one recognized the janitor behind the genial Santa

119

mask, as he began calling names and handing out gifts. I realized that this tree and the gift under it would be all the Christmas little Louise would know. Her eyes were dancing and she could hardly keep her seat for excitement as she listened eagerly for her name to be called.

The boys were excited, too. They knew which name Walter had drawn and they were curious to see what he had done about it. He was anxious, too---to prove to his buddies that he had no affection for the person whose name he had drawn.

Finally Santa called "Louise." She almost climbed over herself to get out of her seat and to claim her present. Each gift, so far, had been a nice one.

The sound of snickering among the boys stopped and all eyes were on Louise as she was handed the little square box. Nervously she began unwrapping the package. Suddenly a feeling of real joy filled every heart as we saw the wonderful expression of happiness and surprise that came to Louise's face as she lifted her gift from its box.

"A doll," she whispered, cuddling it to her and rocking it tenderly in her arms as she returned to her seat, where she continued to pour out upon it all the love and affection for which she so earnestly yearned.

To Louise the doll was not a gift from anyone---rather the Miracle of the Christmas Tree.

To the rest of us, it was the Miracle of Christmas! A dramatization of the fact that it is blessed to make someone happy. No one had really meant to hurt or be unkind. Hazel, in her remembering "one of the least of these," had made it possible for the true spirit of Christmas to be magnified in every heart that day.

It was as though our little Louise had become the Christ Child before our very eyes.

"A Gift for Louise," Pearl B. Mason. *Christmas I Remember Best*, Salt Lake City, Utah. Deseret News Publishing Company, 1983, 23. © Deseret News Publishing Company, reprinted courtesy of Deseret News Publishing Company.

I Knew You Would Come

ELIZABETH KING ENGLISH

Herman and I locked our general store and dragged ourselves home. It was 11:00 p.m. on Christmas Eve of 1949. We were dog-tired. We had sold almost all of our toys; and all of the layaways, except one package, had been picked up. Usually we kept the store open until everything had been claimed. We wouldn't have woken up happy on Christmas knowing that some child's gift was still on the layaway shelf. But the person who had put a dollar down on that package never returned.

Early Christmas morning, we and our twelve-year-old son, Tom, opened gifts. But I'll tell you, there was something humdrum about this Christmas. Tom was growing up; I missed his childish exuberance of past years.

As soon as breakfast was over, Tom left to visit his friend next door. Herman mumbled, "I'm going back to sleep. There's nothing left to stay up for." So, there I was alone, feeling let down.

And then it began. A strange, persistent urge. It seemed to be telling me to go to the store. I looked at the sleet and icy sidewalk outside. That's crazy, I said to myself. I tried dismissing the urge, but it wouldn't leave me alone. In fact, it was getting stronger. Finally, I couldn't stand it any longer, and I got dressed.

Outside, the wind cut right through me, and the sleet stung my cheeks. I groped my way to the store, slipping and sliding. In front stood two boys, one about nine and the other six. What in the world?

"See, I told you she would come!" the older boy said jubilantly. The younger one was wet with tears. When he saw me, his sobbing stopped.

"What are you two doing out here?" I scolded, hurrying them into the store.

"You should be at home on a day like this!" They were poorly dressed. They had no hats or gloves, and their shoes were barely held together. I rubbed their icy hands and got them up close to the heater.

A DECEMBER TO REMEMBER

"We've been waiting for you," replied the older boy.

"My little brother, Jimmy, didn't get any Christmas." He touched Jimmy's shoulder. "We wanted to buy some skates. That's what he wants. We have these three dollars," he said, pulling the bills from his pocket.

I looked at the money. I looked at their expectant faces, and then I looked around the store. "I'm sorry," I said, "but we have no—" Then my eye caught sight of the layaway shelf with its lone package. "Wait a minute," I told the boys. I walked over, picked up the package, unwrapped it, and miracle; there was a pair of skates!

Jimmy reached for them. Lord, let them be his size. And miracle added upon miracle; they were his size.

The older boy presented the dollars to me. "No," I told him, "I want you to have these skates, and I want you to use your money to get some gloves." The boys just blinked at first. Then their eyes became like saucers, and their grins stretched wide when they understood I was giving them the skates. What I saw in Jimmy's eyes was a blessing. It was pure joy, and it was beautiful. My spirit rose.

We walked out together, and as I locked the door, I turned to the older brother and said, "How did you know I would come?"

I wasn't prepared for his reply. His gaze was steady, and he answered me softly. "I asked Jesus to send you."

The tingles in my spine weren't from the cold. God had planned this. As we waved goodbye, I turned home to a brighter Christmas.

Handfuls of Pennies

ELLA BIRDIE JAMISON, AS TOLD TO NORMA FAVOR

Ella was disillusioned.

This year, even the lighted candles shining from the evergreen-trimmed windows, the sound of sleigh bells, and the laughter of children sledding on the snow-covered hills had failed to bring Ella the usual Christmas expectation.

It was Christmas Eve in the little town of Beetown, Wisconsin. Her twin brother, Buzz, was sledding in the moonlight with his boisterous friends. Mother was tending the telephone switchboard located on their kitchen wall, and right now, Ella had no idea where her father was or what he was doing. Earlier, she had helped him wait on customers in their little store below their apartment. When the last customer had left the building, Papa had locked the store door and sent Ella upstairs. Now she gazed out of the window of the upstairs parlor at the snow-covered town below and hoped Papa would come upstairs and grab her in his usual bear hug and laugh her out of her melancholy.

Ella glanced at the wrapped presents underneath the Christmas tree and sighed. Weeks ago, she had helped Papa unpack the Christmas merchandise and place the toys, books, and games on the store shelves. She had looked at and touched every potential present, and she knew some of it was under the tree with her name tagged on it. She wished that just once she would be surprised with a wonderful gift that she had never laid eyes on. When she had shared her thoughts with Papa tonight, he had just looked at her with twinkling eyes and smiled. Just thinking of his amusement at her misery made her so mad that she stamped her high-button shoes and flounced to the horsehair sofa, her long black braid switching angrily.

As she sat pouting, she heard noises coming from the store below. Cautiously, she crept down the stairway and opened the door a crack. In the near dark, she saw someone at the till. The sound of clinking coins fell softly in the silent store. Ella gasped in dismay as the large dark shape turned. It was Papa! Why was Papa stealing from the till? And why was he dressed so strange? Amazement and a trickle of fear flushed her chubby cheeks.

Papa paused for a moment as if considering something and then beckoned her over to him. Silently, he handed her a handful of small brown-paper bags. He showed her how to put a handful of pennies into each of the bags while he put on a red velvet jacket trimmed with white fur and a red, tasseled velvet hat. Ella exclaimed that he looked just like Santa Claus. Papa only winked and told her to run and put on her warmest hat, coat, and her muff. He was going somewhere, and she was coming with him. In a wink, Ella was back. Before she could take another breath, Papa had her snuggled in their sleigh amid boxes filled with turkey-dinner fixings. The box of penny-filled paper bags sat between them.

With a toss of his mane, their horse trotted away, pulling the sleigh quietly through the snow. No one saw them slip down the short, snow-covered main street and out onto the country road. Ella was speechless. It was all so magical. As they approached a shabby little shack, she heard the laughter and cries of little children. Papa put his finger to his lip and gave her a little bag of pennies to carry. He hoisted a large box of groceries, and they sidled up to the sagging porch. Papa put the box close to the door and motioned Ella to run back to the sleigh. Papa slowly and quietly opened the front door of the house and tossed the bag of pennies as far into the room as he could and then raced to the sleigh and whipped the horse into a fast trot. As they flew away, she heard delighted screams of joy. Papa beamed at the sound, and Ella felt the stirring of something magical.

For the next few hours, they sped from house to house.

After the sleigh was empty, they headed back to the store. Papa strode in, lit as many lamps as he could, and opened up the store for business. A few children were already waiting on the porch, shivering in their thin coats. Each child clutched a small paper bag of pennies.

Ella's heart gave a lurch when she noticed that Papa had lowered all the prices on the toys and candy. She looked at the children, and her smile knew no bounds. She had never heard such a wonderful commotion as those children made as they spent their pennies. Nor had she ever seen such happiness. Her heart was filled with joy and pride. She looked at each child, and then she raised her gaze to her father's beaming face. That Christmas, Papa had given her the best gift of all. He had shared with her the gift of giving.

"Handful of Pennies," Ella Birdie Jamison, as told to Norma Favor. Permission to print granted by the author.

The Legend of the Christmas Apple

RUTH SAWYER

Once long ago, there lived a little Swiss clock maker by the name of Herman Joseph. He lived alone in a little one-room home next to his clock shop. The clock maker's back was bent, and his legs were crooked, which made him very short and funny to look at. However, there was no kinder face than his in the whole city, and the children loved him. Whenever a toy was broken or a doll lost an arm or a leg, its owner would carry it straight to Herman's shop. Whatever work Herman was doing, he would always put it aside to mend the cherished toy, never taking even a penny for his work.

It was the custom in those days for those who lived in the city to bring gifts to the great cathedral on Christmas and lay them before the large painting of Mary and the Christ Child. There was a saying among them that when a gift was brought that pleased the Christ Child more than any other, He would reach down from Mary's arms and take it. This was but a saying, of course.

Those who had no gifts to bring went to the cathedral just the same on Christmas Eve to see the gifts of the others and to hear the carols and watch the bright candles burn. The little clock maker was one of those. Often he was stopped, and someone would ask, "How does it happen that you never bring a gift? Poorer than you have brought offerings to the Child. Where is your gift?"

Herman answered, "Wait! Someday you will see that I, too, shall bring a gift!" The truth of it was that the little clock maker was always so busy helping the village children, the poor, and the needy, that there was never money left for gifts at Christmas.

He did have one wonderful idea, a secret surprise for the Christ Child, and he worked on it every spare minute he had. It was a clock, the most wonderful and beautiful clock ever made, and every part of it had been fashioned with loving care. He had spent years carving the case and hands, years perfecting the works.

The little clock was fashioned like a stable with rafter, stall, and manger. The Holy Mother knelt beside the manger in which the tiny baby lay, while through the open door of the stable, the hours chimed. There were kings, shepherds, and angels, and when the hour struck, one of the figures knelt in adoration before the sleeping child while silver chimes played. Finally, he had a gift worthy to take to the cathedral. The last days before Christmas, Herman set the Christmas clock in the shop window to the delight of passersby and the children who always visited.

The day before Christmas, Herman cleaned up his shop, wound up all the clocks, brushed his clothes, and checked the Christmas clock one more time. He had to be sure that everything was perfect.

A blind beggar came to his door and, in his usual manner, the old clock maker gave all the money he had to him, reserving a few cents with which to buy an apple for his supper. He was putting the apple away in the cupboard when the door of the shop opened. Trude, a neighbor woman, came in softly crying. "Herr Joseph," she explained, "my husband is very ill. The medicine he needed was so expensive. All the money I had put by for Christmas is gone. How can I tell the children? Already they have lighted the candle at the window and wait for Kris Kringle to come."

The clock maker smiled gently. "Come, dear friend, all will be well. Perhaps I can sell a clock."

He buttoned his coat, picked out the best of the clocks he still had in the shop, and went out. He went to the rich merchants, but their houses were full of clocks. Other craftsmen in the village said the clocks were too old-fashioned. The clock maker even stood on the street corners and in the town square crying, "A clock for sale. A good clock for sale!" No one paid attention to him.

At last, he gathered up his courage and went to the elaborate home of the richest man in the village. "Herr Graff, will your Excellency buy a clock?" He was trembling at his own boldness.

"I would not ask, but it is for Christmas, and I am needing to buy a little happiness for some children."

Herr Graff said, "Yes, I will buy a clock, but I want only the beautiful Christmas clock in your shop window. It must be that clock or none."

"But that is impossible!" exclaimed the clock maker. "Anything but that clock! I have spent years making that clock to give as a gift to the Christ Child." Disheartened, he stumbled out of Herr Graff's house and trudged back to his shop. As he passed Trude's humble home, he saw the children at the window with their lighted candle. He heard their mother singing and saw the hope shining in their eyes.

So, it happened that early on that Christmas evening, the servant of Herr Graff came to the clock maker's shop and carried away the beautiful Christmas clock, and coins were quietly pressed into the hand of his neighbor. As Herman looked out the door, the chimes commenced to ring from the great cathedral, and the streets became noisy with crowds making their way to the church, bearing their offerings.

"I have gone empty handed before," he said sadly. "I can go that way again." He buttoned up his coat and turned to shut his cupboard door, but his eyes caught the shining red apple he had placed there. A smile warmed his face and lighted his eyes. "It is all I have. I will carry that to the Christ Child. It is better than going empty handed."

The great cathedral was full of peace and beauty when Herr Joseph entered. Many gifts were on the altar, richer gifts than had been brought for many years. There were beautifully wrought vessels from the East, songs and poems illustrated on fine parchment, paintings of the saints and angels. After all these offerings had been made, the little clock maker walked slowly up the aisle, holding tightly to his gift of the Christmas apple.

As the people saw, a murmur arose. "Shame! See what he brings? Has he nothing better to give the Christ Child?" The words reached Herman, and he stumbled on, his eyes blinded by his tears. He quickly left his gift and turned to walk back down the aisle. Then the murmur of shame died away, and in its place rose one of wonder and awe. Soon the words became understandable. "The miracle! It has happened!"

All the people knelt in the big cathedral. The little clock maker turned and looked up through tear-dimmed eyes and seemed to see the Christ Child reach down from Mary's arms with outstretched hands to take his gift.

"The Legend of the Christmas Apple," Ruth Sawyer

Boxes Full of Love

HOPE M. WILLIAMS

The fragrant "mountain" odor of the pinion pine Christmas tree; the soft white snow that lay in stillness around our farm home; the frosty window panes with their dainty patterns; the spicy goodness of frying doughnuts; the Christmas carols being sung everywhere; and the thrill of hearing St. Luke's story of the Saviour's birth, "And there were shepherds---" these were all part of the Christmas spirit, which as a child I had called my "good feeling," and now whenever I experience these things again, I start remembering...

Many of our Christmases then were very meager, and the things that are considered musts in most homes today were absent from our festivities, but the "feeling" was always so much present in our home that I never remember feeling too disappointed when "hoped for" things did not materialize.

The Christmas that comes most vividly to my mind was one of those meager ones. My twin sister, June, and I were about 10 years old, I think, and were painfully aware that Christmas gifts this year would be few. We were too young to know the real concern as our parents and our older sisters did, but there seemed to be less gaiety than usual this year, and we felt it keenly.

So, in our eagerness to keep this happy "feeling," and because we had no money with which to buy gifts, June and I thought it would be fun to pretend we had a nice gift for Mother.

We wrapped up an empty small box, placed it in another empty box; then we wrapped it in green paper and tied it with a big wide red ribbon. It was the first package to be placed under the tree.

We were very pleased at first when Mother showed such interest in it, but when she keep looking at it and saying "ah---hmm?" in that cute way of hers, the closer it came to Christmas, the more we wished that we had something---just something---in it. We even lay awake at night whispering and wishing we could think of something really wonderful to put in that box! Finally we came up with the idea of putting a letter in it---a special one to her from us.

Christmas morning finally came, and Mother was still so curious about the package that my heart sank and I wished heartily that we had never thought of such an idea. When she asked to open the big package first, I was more miserable than ever.

June was miserable too, because she kept saying over and over, "It's really nothing, Mama," but Mother kept peeling off paper and raising her eyes in questions as each box only proved to be outside another one.

"We were just fixing a kind of surprise," I said, miserably.

"My! Just look at this! Another box to open?" said Mother, with a smile on her face as more wrappings came off.

My pain was so acute by then that I remember trying to grab the box, tear the rest of the wrappings off and get it over with, but everyone kept saying, "Leave her alone, it's her gift," and "don't be so rude," mistaking my misery for my eagerness to have mother see what we had given her.

As the last box was unwrapped and the lid lifted off, I uttered one final plea, "We wish it were something really good, Mama."

There in the bottom of the last small box lay a folded piece of paper on which was written:

"Dear Mama,

We don't have a present to give you, but we are going to try to be better girls so you won't have to feel bad when you scold us and everything."

Love,

Hope and June."

Mother looked up from the paper with tears in her eyes, and with a dear sweet look on her face she said, "That's the nicest gift my girls could give me."

I have had the feeling ever since, that no gift, no matter how costly, could ever be quite wonderful enough for such a mother!"

"Boxes Full of Love," Hope M. Williams, *Christmas I Remember Best,* Salt Lake City, Deseret News Publishing, 1983. © Deseret News Publishing Company, reprinted courtesy of Deseret News Publishing Company.

Bethann's Christmas Prayer

MARILYN MORGAN HELLEBERG

"Put that doll down!" growled Mrs. Skorp, owner of Willow Creek's only store. "You'll break her!"

"Oh no," said Bethann. "I wouldn't hurt her. I love her!"

"Love her, do you?" Well, you'd better get over that in a hurry." Mrs. Skorp whisked the doll out of Bethann's arms. "That's the most expensive doll in the store, and with your dad laid off."

"It's o.k.," said Bethann, her wistful brown eyes scanning the drawn face of the middle-aged shopkeeper. "I won't touch her again until she's mine. She's my Christmas prayer!"

"Oh? I suppose you've been talking to Jesus again?"

"Why, yes! I have!" Bethann's pale, plain looking face took on a sudden glow. "Last night, I talked to Him a long time---and when I went to sleep, an angel with golden wings floated down on a cloud and told me I could have one Christmas prayer answered this year. I could have anything I asked for---but only one thing. I've asked for Betsy."

"Betsy!"

"Yes, that's what I've named her."

Mrs. Skorp tossed her hands over her head and walked away. "Angels now!" she muttered.

By the time she got home, Bethann was near to tears. "I can't stand her, Mommie! Mrs. Skorp is the meanest lady in the whole world!"

"Don't be too hard on her, dear," said her mother. "Mrs. Skorp used to be a very nice lady before the accident."

"The accident?"

"Yes. It was before you were born. The Skorps were driving home from Kansas City, after spending Christmas with relatives, when they hit a patch of ice and went off the road.

130

Mr. Skorp was killed instantly, and their baby daughter died a couple of days later. Mrs. Skorp wasn't even hurt---at least, her body wasn't."

"I didn't even know she had a baby," said Bethann, fingering the hem of her skirt.

"After that, Mrs. Skorp just kind of dried up. She stopped going anywhere, closed herself off from everybody, even quit going to church. Some say she's been mad at God ever since."

"I've never heard of anyone being mad at God," said Bethann.

At bedtime, she knelt down and started talking with her Friend. "Lord, You know Mrs. Skorp---the one with the pinched up face and the screechy voice? You probably haven't heard from her lately because, well, I guess she's been mad at You for a long time. Anyway, Jesus, I've been thinking, and I've figured out a way to get her over being mad at You. So if You don't mind, I'd like to take back that Christmas prayer for my Betsy doll. Instead, Lord, would You please send Mrs. Skorp a new baby girl? Then maybe she won't be mad at You anymore. Thank You, Jesus."

After school the next day, Bethann stopped at the store again, only this time, she was very careful to not even look at Betsy.

"Mrs. Skorp, I talked to Jesus again last night. . ." The tall, gaunt lady grunted and turned away, but Bethann continued. "I asked Him to give you a new baby girl."

"You WHAT?!" said Mrs. Skorp, wheeling around. "You really have lost your senses! Besides, if there is a God, He sure doesn't answer prayers. Now you get home!"

On the day before Christmas, Bethann made a paper card for Mrs. Skorp. The shopkeeper was alone in the store when Bethann tiptoed in. The woman was staring at a framed picture, clutching it so tightly Bethann saw that her knuckles were white.

"I brought you a Christmas card, Mrs. Skorp." Surprised, the woman laid the picture on the counter and reached for the card. She opened it and read the childish scrawl: "Jesus loves you. And so do I. Bethann."

Mrs. Skorp coughed and turned away. That was when Bethann sneaked a look at the picture on the counter. She saw a beautiful, smiling young woman holding a curly haired baby in her arms.

"Is that your baby that died?" asked Bethann.

Mrs. Skorp slumped into the old library chair and put her head in her hands. "Her name was Betsy," she said. Bethann stared at her. The woman's body began to shake as deep, low sobs poured out of her. The little girl tiptoed over and put her hand timidly on Mrs. Skorp's knee.

"I asked Jesus to send you a new little girl to love," said Bethann. "Are you crying because He didn't answer my prayer?"

"No," said Mrs. Skorp. She scooped Bethann up into her lap, pressing the little head close to her heart and rocking back and forth, back and forth, in the straight chair.

"No, my little . . . darling. "I'm crying because . . .because He did."

"Bethann's Christmas Prayer," Marilyn Morgan Helleberg. Permission to reprint granted by Robert King, her husband.

Angels, Once in a While

BARB IRWIN

In September 1960, I woke up one morning with six hungry babies and just 75 cents in my pocket. Their father was gone. The boys ranged from three months to seven years; their sister was two.

Their dad had never been much more than a presence they feared. Whenever they heard his tires crunch on the gravel driveway they would scramble to hide under their beds. He did manage to leave 15 dollars a week to buy groceries.

Now that he had decided to leave, there would be no more beatings, but no food either. If there was a welfare system in effect in southern Indiana at that time, I certainly knew nothing about it.

I scrubbed the kids until they looked brand new and then put on my best homemade dress. I loaded them into the rusty old '51 Chevy and drove off to find a job. The seven of us went to every factory, store, and restaurant in our small town. No luck. The kids stayed, crammed into the car and tried to be quiet while I tried to convince whomever would listen that I was willing to learn or do anything. I had to have a job. Still no luck.

The last place we went to, just a few miles out of town, was an old Root Beer Barrel drive-in that had been converted to a truck stop. It was called the Big Wheel. An old lady named Granny owned the place and she peeked out of the window from time to time at all those kids. She needed someone on the graveyard shift, 11 at night until seven in the morning. She paid 65 cents an hour and I could start that night.

I raced home and called the teenager down the street that babysat for people. I bargained with her to come and sleep on my sofa for a dollar a night. She could arrive with her pajamas on and the kids would already be asleep. This seemed like a good arrangement to her, so we made a deal. That night when the little ones and I knelt to say our prayers we all thanked God for finding Mommy a job.

And so I started at the Big Wheel. When I got home in the mornings I woke the baby-sitter up and sent her home with one dollar of my tip money--fully half of what I averaged every night. As the weeks went by, heating bills added another strain to my meager wage. The tires on the old Chevy had the consistency of penny balloons and began to leak. I had to fill them with air on the way to work and again every morning before I could go home.

One bleak fall morning, I dragged myself to the car to go home and found four tires in the back seat. New tires! There was no note, no nothing, just those beautiful brand-new tires. Had angels taken up residence in Indiana? I wondered. I made a deal with the owner of the local service station. In exchange for his mounting the new tires, I would clean up his office. I remember it took me a lot longer to scrub his floor than it did for him to do the tires.

I was now working six nights instead of five and it still wasn't enough. Christmas was coming and I knew there would be no money for toys for the kids. I found a can of red paint and started repairing and painting some old toys. Then I hid them in the basement so there would be something for Santa to deliver on Christmas morning. Clothes were a worry, too. I was sewing patches on top of patches on the boys' pants, and soon they would be too far-gone to repair.

On Christmas Eve, the usual customers were drinking coffee in the Big Wheel. These were the truckers, Les, Frank, and Jim, and a state trooper named Joe. A few musicians were hanging around after a gig at the American Legion and were dropping nickels in the pinball machine. The regulars all just sat around and talked through the wee hours of the morning and then left to get home before the sun came up.

When it was time for me to go home at seven o'clock on Christmas morning I hurried to the car. I was hoping the kids wouldn't wake up before I managed to get home and get the presents from the basement and place them under the tree. (We had cut down a small cedar tree by the side of the road down by the dump.)

It was still dark and I couldn't see much, but there appeared to be some dark shadows in the car--or was that just a trick of the night? Something certainly looked different, but it was hard to tell what. When I reached the car, I peered warily into one of the side windows. Then my jaw dropped in amazement. My old battered Chevy was full--full to the top with boxes of all shapes and sizes. I quickly opened the driver's side door, scrambled inside and kneeled in the front facing the back seat. Reaching back, I pulled off the lid of the top box. Inside was a whole case of little blue jeans, sizes 2-10! I looked inside another box: It was full of shirts to go with the jeans. Then I peeked inside some of the other boxes. There were candy and nuts and bananas and bags of groceries. There was an enormous ham for baking, and canned vegetables and potatoes. There was pudding and Jell-O and cookies, pie filling and flour. There was a whole bag of laundry supplies and cleaning items. And there were five toy trucks and one beautiful little doll.

As I drove back through empty streets as the sun slowly rose on the most amazing Christmas Day of my life, I was sobbing with gratitude. And I will never forget the joy on the faces of my little ones that precious morning.

Yes, there were angels in Indiana that long-ago December. And they all hung out at the Big Wheel truck stop.

Away in a Manger: A Missionary Christmas

P. DAVID SONNTAG

It was my last Christmas in the mission field. I was serving in Tehuacan, a midsized city in southern Mexico. During that autumn, I had enjoyed training a new young missionary named Elder Martinez. We had worked hard and been well received, but in the days leading up to Christmas, it became more difficult to find people to teach. Everyone seemed busy with their holiday preparations. Though happy to be serving the Lord, we had thoughts of home as Christmas Day approached. As we walked the streets contemplating where to go and who to visit, we passed by an outdoor market.

It was nearing dusk and in the exposed bulb lighting of the market, we could see bright piñatas and small toys and smell cider for sale. We thought of Maria and Patricia Gonzalez, a mother and daughter who had recently accepted the gospel and been baptized. We had interacted with them at church but had never been to visit them, because the only place they could afford to live was a far-flung collection of houses on a hillside well outside the city.

Patricia had two beautiful young daughters, both under the age of five that she was raising with the help of her mother. As we walked through the market those children came to our mind and everything we saw seemed liked something those kids needed. We spent the extra money that we had on toys, candy, a piñata and two Santa hats that turned white shirted missionaries into elves. The next day was Christmas Eve.

We found directions to their home and boarded a bus to travel the hour that it takes to reach the closest stop to their hillside. Upon disembarking we started trudging up the double track road with rain pouring down from above and a river a water flowing between our feet. We walked for a while trying to find their home on unmarked dirt roads and paths, with some effort and after asking, we found it. Their home was a 10x10 foot stick hut with a tin roof. We knocked expectantly, but no one was home. Not wanting to return without delivering our gifts, we decided to wait.

We could think of nothing else to do on a rainy Christmas Eve and so headed up the trail that led up the small ravine toward the mountain behind their hut. As we walked along the thin trail, the rain stopped and the afternoon sunlight shone down on us and lit up a beautiful, glistening scene of tall cactus and green shrubs. We walked quietly along enjoying the warmth of the sun and of each other's company and a new optimism that the peaceful scene had brought us.

As the sun sank low in the horizon, we headed back toward their hut. When we emerged from the ravine, we saw light shining through the cracks between the sticks that made up the wall of their home. We began singing Christmas carols as we approached and were greeted by two pairs of children's smiling eyes that peered out of the open door toward us. We were quickly invited in and asked to sit with them on the only furniture in their stick home, the one bed, which they all shared. We happily imparted our simple gifts, which were received with so much excitement by the children.

We sang and enjoyed one another's company and remembered the birth of the Savior. As we sang in Spanish, "Away in a Manger" the words and spirit touched me.

"Be near me, Lord Jesus; I ask thee to stay

Close by me forever, and love me, I pray.

Bless all the dear children in thy tender care,

And fit us for heaven, to live with thee there."

My thoughts turned to the first Christmas and the humble circumstances of the Savior's birth. I, too, was celebrating Christmas in humble circumstances. I, too, was witness to great love. I was with women who loved their children no less than Mary did Jesus. I could feel of the love of our Savior for that humble family. I recognized the love the Savior showed me as I walked with my companion on the sunlit hillside above their home. I thanked my Savior for allowing me to be a messenger of love that Christmas.

Used by Permission of the Author.

Christmas Spirit

STEPHANIE L. JENSEN (age 11)

Long ago, when Christmas was a feeling and not a gift. I wanted a teddy bear, soft and cuddly. My parents were farmers and they didn't have a lot of money. For Christmas we would get things like oranges, peppermint sticks, and a new coat that my mother would make for us every year. But nothing expensive. I had to take the chicken's eggs to the general store, even though I was just little. That was my job.

Around Christmastime the window of the general store in town was a child's dream with dolls, bears, trains, and candy. There, sitting near the front of the window was my bear. I wanted it so bad. It looked just like a cub. It was soft, not rough like all the woolen stockings I had to wear. When I would take the eggs to the store I would sit outside the window and just stare at the bear with the big red bow.

My older brother, Simon, had one that looked just like the one in the window. He had saved all of his money for a whole year just to buy it. He loved that bear so much; he would take it everywhere but would be careful not to get it dirty. Sometimes when he wasn't home I would sneak into his room and hold the bear like a baby. But I had to be careful because if my older brother saw me with the bear he would get very angry.

So every time I got home from the long cold walk from the general store I would tell my mother about the bear. My mother would just smile and nod. She never acted interested in the bear. I never knew why.

Finally on Christmas Eve night we acted out the story of the manger scene. I just knew Santa Claus would later come down the chimney, pull down my thin stocking, and put a beautiful bear inside. I couldn't sleep all night.

At about one o'clock I heard someone creep down the stairs and I heard them by the Christmas tree. Then I got up and looked for Santa. In place of Santa was my older brother climbing the stairs.

"What are you doing awake?" he asked. "Santa won't come if you're awake. Go back to bed."

My brother seemed angry but he had a strange twinkle in his eye. I crawled back in bed. The next thing I knew, my younger brother Jimmy was shaking me to get up. I was the middle child. I had to take care of my younger siblings but deal with my older brother as well.

"Santa Claus came!" he shouted. I got up and ran downstairs. There sitting under the tree was a crudely wrapped present.

Then my brother Jimmy and I had to wake everyone up. Everyone seemed especially tired this time except Simon. He jumped right out of bed and ran down to look at the presents.

Finally we were able to get everyone out of bed and ready to open their presents. We looked in the stockings and saw things like peppermint sticks and pencils. Then we opened up the beautiful coats made by my mother. They were all so neatly stitched. Our father had written each of us a letter. My parents were always smiling on Christmas, but a look of sadness filled their eyes.

"Looks like Judith was extra good this year," Jimmy said. "There is a big present under the tree for her." I took the brown package in my arms, holding it like a baby. I gently unwrapped the gift, and inside was the beautiful teddy bear I had wanted. I hugged the bear for what seemed like forever, Santa had brought my bear!

I looked over at Simon. His eyes welled with tears. He wasn't carrying his beloved bear. He usually slept with it in his arms and took it with him to breakfast. But his arms were empty. I then understood that Santa lives in my older brother and all who carry the true meaning of Christmas.

Used by Permission of the Author.

The Gift of a Lighted Tree

ALISON R. DUNN

To start this story, I need to tell you about my husband's love of Christmas lights. He loves Christmas lights, not in the crazy, over the top, stop and watch my synchronized light and music display, but a tasteful decoration of a few strands on the house and on the tress. Nothing fancy, but I think, to him, this is Christmas.

If he had been an engineer or an electrician, the end of the year may have provided him with some time to decorate as he sees fit for Christmas. But he is an accountant, a corporate accountant, and unfortunately, Christmas falls very close to the end of the year. This is the busiest time of the year for most people, but especially for him. Nights are too long, mornings too early, sleep is seldom, and pressure is intense. Most years, his Christmas shopping is done late on Christmas Eve, and some years, it is a note expressing a present that he hoped to buy.

We had recently moved into our first house. It was a beautiful house in a lovely neighborhood on the hill. We were so excited about having our own home and being there for our first Christmas. Outside of this house was a huge pine tree, perfectly shaped and visible all the way down the street. Months before Christmas arrived, I heard talk of how beautiful this tree would look all lit up for Christmas. But as Christmas got closer and closer, I realized there was no time for him to get up and do the lights on our house, let alone on this gigantic tree.

I, who have been taught by my mother to love Christmas, had been planning and preparing for months. All the presents for our four young children, all under the age of six, had been bought months ago. But what to get my husband for Christmas had eluded me; I could think of much that he needed but nothing that he wanted. Nothing he or I could really be excited about.

It was only a week before Christmas, late one night as I walked outside to pick up the mail and to have a moment of peace (remember the four kids under six), and I looked at the big tree and thought, it's too bad he never got time to light that tree. That was the one thing he wanted for Christmas.

Wait, that was it, the one thing he wanted for Christmas. I knew what I had to do, but how?

This was a huge tree, and even if we had a ladder that would reach that high, there was not a way to prop it up. It was a large bushy tree. How was I going to light this tree? I thought and planned it all that night. I would use the A-frame ladder we had to help me through the first couple passes, but after that, I was going to have to find some other way to string the lights that high.

The next day, I headed to the hardware store where I bought lots of lights, a twenty-foot PVC pipe, and a hook. Late that night, when all the kids were asleep, and it was too dark for the neighbors to see and wonder what I was doing, I headed out with a twenty-foot pole with a hook attached to the end. It was a windy night, which was often the case for this house on the hill, but it was a gorgeous moonlit night. This was a brilliant plan, and after the next few passes around the tree, I realized a PVC pole was not that easy to maneuver when stretched straight up over my head; it tended to move and bend quite a bit, and the wind was not really helping matters. But, it was looking fabulous, and what a surprise it was going to be as he headed down our road, late, late that night, and saw that big tree at the end of the road, all lit up for Christmas.

Unfortunately, two problems arose. One, I had run out of lights, because it was a big tree. Two, I had run out of pole. I still had about fifteen to twenty feet left to light the very top. And how would that look, a tree only decorated on the bottom half? Well, I was determined to try some more. I hid my tracks and waited until the next day to run to the hardware store to try to figure out how to get the top finished. I walked the hardware store for a long time, but I couldn't come up with a way to extend the pole. Adding more PVC pipe would have made it too wobbly, and it was barely working at twenty feet. The only thing I could think of was adding a wooden handle to the end. So, buying a broom handle and ten more strings of lights, I headed home to finish my tree.

That night, unfortunately, was more windy; OK, a lot more windy. It was only a couple of days before Christmas, and if I didn't get them up now, then what was the point? I put the kids to bed and headed out to the tree once the lights next door were out. If watching me last night had been funny, this night would have been hilarious. I stuffed the broom handle up the pole, but it was too small, and it just went right inside. How was I going to do this? Thinking quickly, I grabbed an old sock, wrapped it around the tip of the broom handle, and stuffed it in. It worked! It wasn't perfect, it was still very wobbly, but it added a good five feet to the pole. That would be enough, right?

Four strands down, just the top of the tree to go, but again, the pole ran out. It wasn't long enough, and I was so close. I was standing out there late at night, in the cold and wind, waving a twenty-five-foot pole over my head and trying desperately to get the lights up the tree and praying desperately that they didn't pull apart at the plug connections, because there would be no way to reconnect them.

I thought about giving up. It still didn't look done; the top was still very bare. I had to find a way to get those last ten feet. So, out came the ladder, the little A-frame ladder with the sign on the top two steps that says you shouldn't stand up there. Well, I did. I stood on the top of that ladder, with a twenty-foot PVC pipe and broom handle stuffed into it with a sock keeping the two attached and tried with all my might to light that top of the tree. It wasn't safe, it wasn't sane, it probably didn't make a difference, but I did it.

And when I plugged in that tree for the first time, tears coming from my eyes, imaging his surprise as he drove down our road and three o'clock in the morning, I felt what it was to give a true gift, a gift of sacrifice and love, a gift of myself.

Used by Permission of the Author.

A Red Bike

STEPHANIE L. JENSEN

I lay flat on my back, looking at the ceiling with a headache. My head was sore from the rag curls my mom rolled into my frizzy hair last night to smooth it down for Christmas Day. I rolled over, arms spread out and one of my relaxed arms came down on Mary's head.

"Ouch" said my one-year-older and not-so-wiser sister Mary. She always bossed me around.

She turned her head, also in tight curls, and buried her face into the pillow.

"We have to go back to sleep so Santa will come," she said, pulling the covers back over her head and pretending to snore. I laughed and began tickling her in the center of her armpit. She laughed so hard she squirmed her way off the layered corduroy quilt onto the thin carpet. Mary leapt back into bed and for a few chaotic seconds, and legs and elbows appeared and disappeared from the thick of the blanket accompanied by our delighted squeals.

Suddenly we heard the wooden clank of cowboy boot footsteps coming down the stairs. I rolled over and shut my eyes closed as if I had been peacefully sleeping for hours. Mary did the same. A hand slowly pushed the door open and an olive-skinned face peaked around the door, wearing thick black-rimmed glasses and a suit from the church meeting he had just attended. My dad didn't say anything. He seldom did. He gently walked over to our bed and examined our faces to make sure they were shut.

"Humph," he said, knowing we had been awake only seconds earlier. Dad turned around and walked out of the room and firmly shut the door. After a few minutes, I could hear my sister's slow breaths and every so often a slight snore. I began to try to fall asleep; I counted sheep and moved my hot feet to the edge of the bed. Every so often I heard rustling upstairs. I was seven years old and I wasn't sure I believed in Santa but hung up my stocking just in case. We always had our basic needs met, and Mom and Dad seemed to make do with what we had, but I didn't get new dresses as often as my friends did. Dad didn't drive a fancy car, either.

This year, Mary and I wanted the same Christmas present. I knew Santa—if he was real—might not get it for me, because Santa couldn't always get us the presents we wanted. Mom and Dad told us there were too many kids for everyone to get exactly what they wanted. I hoped with all of my seven year old heart I would get my gift, but I didn't want to be disappointed so I kept most of the wishing to myself.

I woke up to the clock. It said 6:30 a.m. I folded back the covers and shook my sister. "Wake up," I said. "Let's see what Santa brought us." Mary pried her eyes open and looked at me with a red eye. She shook her head and touched her delicate toes to the cold ground. Both of us draped quilts around our necks and ran to wake up our sleepy siblings. Jane, our younger sister, woke right up and danced around the room when we told her Santa had come, her wispy blond hair swaying as she did a series of turns and leaps. Then we worked on our teenage siblings. We pulled their hair, poked their cheeks, and stripped off their blankets. By the time we got to our parents' room, they were tiredly sitting up in bed.

"Let's go see what Santa brought," I said, pulling on my mom's limp hand. I walked down into the kitchen, shivering in my hooded blanket while Mom and Dad checked to see if Santa had indeed brought presents. They called for us to come in and see for ourselves. We walked out, and I stopped in shock. There, sitting next to the tree, was a cinnamon-red bike. It had a bow on it and the tag said it was for Mary and Rebecca. I grabbed Mary's hand, and we danced a celebratory dance in the middle of the room. My dad held the bike up while I sat on the seat. I touched every feature of the bike, checking out all of the pedals and the brakes. I silently noticed that the bike had a few scratches on it, and the pedals had been worn. It wasn't a new bike. I looked at my parents who were standing, arms locked together with the expression of hope and anticipation. I pretended not to notice.

I wrapped my pudgy arms around both of my parents' legs and squeezed. Then I got on the bike with Mary, and we rode around the streets all afternoon, overjoyed at the new world we were exploring.

It wasn't until years later that I understood their sacrifice. I don't remember either of them getting presents on Christmas Day. They had spent all of their money giving the incalculable gift of their hearts.

Used by Permission of the Author.

A Friend

RUTHIE DUNN, AS TOLD BY HER MOTHER

Ruthie has always taken seriously the Christmas challenges given to her by her grandparents. These challenges are difficult for her and push her beyond her level of comfort, and because she really thinks about each one, she seems to have experienced more growth and had more special experiences than some of her siblings.

Some memorable examples are the time she was asked to go through her toys and pick toys that were still in good condition that someone else would enjoy more. Tears were immediately shed as she begged, "Please, Mom, I need all of my toys."

For Ruthie, her toys are a part of her, she knows where she got each one, and each one has a memory attached to it. It is difficult for her to part with each one.

Finally, a pile started to form; however, it consisted mostly of toys of her siblings and a few fast-food toys or toys missing pieces. We sat down and discussed what it might be like to not have any toys to open on Christmas. I asked her to again go through her toys and to think about what she would like to open on Christmas. She took this to heart. The crying didn't stop but the questions did.

Soon, a new pile of "in-good-condition toys" and "toys you would like to receive" began to develop. Later that day, she asked me, "Mom, when are we taking these toys to the shelter?"

"On Saturday, why?" I asked, thinking she was still deciding if she could part with certain items or wondering if I needed to have another talk with her about how much the kids in the shelter would appreciate being able to have some of her toys.

Ruthie surprised me when she said, "I have been thinking about living in a shelter without toys, and I want to earn some money so I can buy some new things to include with my old toys."

Needless to say, tears were falling down both of our faces.

But Ruthie's most special experience from a Christmas challenge occurred when she was in first grade. She was just about to turn seven. The challenge was to find someone who needed some cheering and give them a small Christmas treat. Trying to get my children to focus on someone other than their best friends, I asked each child to write down a list of all the people they knew, not just the people they considered their friends.

That night, I found the lists. Her sister's list had about thirty kids on it, mostly classmates and church friends. However, Ruthie's list was jammed with hundreds of names of everyone she had met, even if she couldn't remember their name. In minute seven-year-old handwriting were names of friends, home teachers, neighbors, ward members, secretaries, receptionists, dentists, etc. I couldn't believe how much thought and how many people she had remembered. There were names in every space and corner of this single sheet of paper.

The next morning, I asked both girls to spend time considering and praying about the list. "Go through this list, and see if any name keeps sticking out to you. Pray about it."

Then, on the next day, Ruthie quietly pulled me aside and told me she had picked a person to give her treat to. "Mom," she said with tears running down her face. "I think Emily really needs it. I can't get her out of my mind."

Tears began forming in my eyes. As a mom, I knew how special it was for Ruthie to have picked this girl. This was a girl that had brought tears to Ruthie's eyes, and I could remember the days Ruthie had come home from school crying because Emily seemed not to like Ruthie very much and would occasionally say something mean or not include her in playground games.

That night, Ruthie and I headed over to Emily's house, and we put the small treat in her mailbox. I can't say that something amazing happened to Emily, although it may have, but I can say that I saw the Christ-like spirit of Christmas radiate in my seven-year-old that Christmas. There is no denying to Ruthie or to me that the spirit directed a young girl to do something nice for a girl who had not "deserved" the kindness in return. I am forever proud of my Ruthie for listening to the spirit and really finding someone who needed a little cheering that Christmas.

Used by Permission of the Author.

Rudolph's Light

STEPHANIE L. JENSEN (age 14)

We all know the Santa Claus version of Rudolph, but do we really know the reason Rudolph's nose is red?

It started like this. More than anything, Rudolph wanted to pull Santa's sleigh. It would be the highlight of Christmas this year. But this year, Rudolph wouldn't be leading the sleigh; in fact, he would be at the very back, since he didn't have a lot of experience.

The day before Christmas Eve, the whole herd of reindeer were grazing the snow-covered plain looking for food. Rudolph thought he saw some uncovered grass in the distance. He was so hungry and set on finding the grassy spot that he didn't notice how far he had strayed from the rest of the herd. He also didn't notice the beautiful snowflakes that were falling. A storm was blowing in. When he finally reached the uncovered grass, the few falling flakes turned into thousands of flakes. Everything turned white, and Rudolph's tracks had been covered by the snow. He couldn't tell which way he had come. It was getting dark, and he had to find shelter from the blizzard. All Rudolph could see was a huge pine tree. The tall tree kept Rudolph dry but far from warm.

The next morning it had stopped snowing. Rudolph was sure he could find his way back now. Besides, wasn't that Santa's workshop there in the far distance? Rudolph galloped off toward the light as quickly as possible. When Rudolph got there, Santa's workshop turned into a tiny village. He looked inside one of the houses. The children were playing with wooden figures. The wooden figures were intricately carved into small people. There was a baby, a young girl, a caring man, and three finely dressed kings carrying gifts, shepherds, sheep, cows, an angel, and a donkey.

Why are all those figures centered around a baby? he wondered. Aren't they too busy to care about a tiny baby? Who is the baby? Endless questions flowed through Rudolph's mind. He looked inside some of the other homes and saw the same figures.

Doesn't anyone around here care about Santa Claus? he thought. And more importantly, the reindeer?

Rudolph was amazed that this baby was special to everyone, even more so than Santa and his reindeer. He decided that when he got home, he would ask Santa about the baby. Surely wise Santa would know the story behind the baby. Rudolph started walking in the direction he thought was Santa's workshop. He walked and walked until his hoofs got sore.

Rudolph saw a star in the distance and began following it. When he got closer, he saw it was another village. In the center of the village stood a large decorated fir tree. It had the normal tinsel and lights on it, but the star was the most beautiful one he had ever seen. It was so bright it practically lit up the whole village. It looked as though someone had reached into the sky and picked out the brightest star.

Rudolph knew that all trees had a star or an angel placed at the very top branch. But why? Why not Santa? Or reindeer, for that matter? Then Rudolph began to wonder who started Christmas. Why is it called Christmas? Why do we give gifts? And what about that baby?

Rudolph was confused and tired. He started to walk. It was already dark, and he was so tired. Rudolph was too tired to notice that the soft snow had turned into grainy sand.

Rudolph came to a stable that was in a cave. Where was he? Rudolph had never left the North Pole before. As Rudolph looked in the cave, he saw the same baby, a shepherd, a young woman, and her husband.

Everyone was praising the baby, saying Savior and King. A king? This is only a small child, how could he be a king? What kind of savior? Rudolph looked into the sky and saw a beautiful star. The star looked exactly like the star on the Christmas tree in the village.

When Rudolph looked back down, the manger scene had disappeared. In its place stood a man with auburn hair. He healed blind men, made lame men walk, and comforted the sick and lonely. Rudolph then saw a riot around the man and a young woman. The man said, "He who hath no sin cast the first stone."

He saw the man in a beautiful garden praying in agony and bleeding. Rudolph heard him say, "Not my will but Thine be done." Then Rudolph saw men spiting on the man and hanging him on a cross.

The painful state of the man hanging on the cross faded back to the manger scene. Tears filled Rudolph's eyes. Now he understood who the baby was and what Christmas is really about, why Santa gives gifts, and why the tiny village had characters that matched the manger scene.

All of a sudden, while Rudolph was staring at the manger and the tiny baby, his nose turned a bright red. Everyone thinks it happened in a lightning storm; let them believe it. The light actually resembles the light of Christ, and it is a light in the darkness. It helps others find their way.

Rudolph suddenly found himself back in his stable. It was Christmas Eve day. It was as if nothing had happened, and then he noticed his nose was still glowing, as it would forever more.

Used by Permission of the Author.

Christmas in the Mojave

PAUL L. SONNTAG

Was it the chance to be like the wise men of old, traveling far distances through the desert at Christmas that made one Christmas so memorable? Was it because we were journeying far from home? Probably not. The real reason it was so memorable was because of whom I spent it with and the special gift of sacrifice that they showed me. It occurred when we abandoned the traditional trappings of the season and spent Christmas on the road.

Traditional Christmas celebrations in my family were usually around a tree with many family members and relatives exchanging gifts and seasonal foods. What fun and excitement we had, but as the years have passed, they all seem to melt together in my memory as ice cream on a warm summer day.

I was a young premedical student and had just started my applications to various medical schools across the country. The competition for admittance to medical school was fierce. I had applied to multiple schools in hopes of entering the following autumn. One elite school on the East Coast was sending a representative to Los Angeles to interview candidates. They invited me, if I could travel to Los Angeles, to meet with him at 9:00 a.m. on the 26th of December. I was excited to go, but I didn't have the money for a plane ticket, so the only option I had was my old secondhand car. Oh, what a Christmas this was going to be, with a long drive to Southern California.

Along came the gift I remember best. I was the only child living at home. My older siblings had moved on their way, and my younger brother was still on a mission. My mother and dad, considering my impending drive, said they wouldn't hear of my driving eight hundred miles alone on Christmas. Since Dad had Christmas Day off, we would get up early on Christmas morning, and the three of us would spend the day in the car. Now, the Mojave Desert, and like country, as seen out of the car window was not a "Currier and Ives" scene but one probably more similar to the one met by the three magi on their journey to the Christ Child.

150

On that long road to California my mom, who said she "had no voice," Dad, who would "try to hold a tune," and I sang Christmas songs. We sang most of the way. Never again would the Christmas carols be the same.

I gained a respect for my parents and what they would do for me, despite what that meant for them. There was no gold or myrrh in the lunch Mom had packed for us, but the gift that was given was a new closeness we had not experienced in a long time.

I don't remember much else of the trip or interview that I had the following day, other than the raised eyebrow when I told him how I had traveled for the appointment. It seems all the other candidates had flown to Los Angeles. Thanks, Mom and Dad, for a real Christmas gift on the birthday of the One who gave the greatest gift of all.

Used by Permission of the Author.

Alvin's Christmas

STEPHANIE L. JENSEN (Age 12)

Once upon a time, in the Appalachian Mountains, there was a little town called Alpine. And in that little town lived a little boy named Alvin. Alvin was twelve years old. He was the oldest child with six younger brothers and sisters. His dad was killed in the war, leaving his mother on her own with only a little money.

Alvin's mom told him there would be no Christmas that year. His mom just could not bring in enough money sewing clothes. Alvin's brothers and sisters were getting excited for Christmas. But whenever they asked Alvin about it, Alvin changed the subject. When he went to church the next Sunday, they learned about giving. Then an idea popped into his head. He could make presents for his brothers and sisters or give them some of his precious things. After helping with Sunday dishes, his brothers and sisters started to make Christmas lists.

Linda wanted a dolly, a bear, and a surprise. John wanted a pocketknife and candy. Michael wanted a bear, candy, and a small tree. Anne wanted a book, a sweater, and candy. Gretchen wanted candy, mittens, and a picture of Santa. Peter wanted a train, a surprise, and a small tree.

Alvin decided he would try to get one thing off of every list and try to get a tree. Sometimes he would get some money, because he helped Mr. Gearly at the grocery store when he could and gave the money to his mom, but sometimes Mr. Gearly would give him some extra money just for him. He had about two dollars. He asked his mom if she could help him. She said she had been saving for Christmas dinner. She had about two dollars, and with Alvin's money, they had four dollars.

Mr. Gearly sold a few trees and knew this family's situation. He decided, even though he was pretty poor himself, to give them a small Christmas tree and some things for Christmas dinner. The next day, he dropped off the presents, knocked on the door of the tiny house, and hid behind a tree. Most of the kids were in school, and the mother opened the door and saw the tree and put away all of the things for Christmas dinner.

She took popcorn and cranberries and strung them around the tree. She found all of her mismatched candles and put them out. But the Christmas tree just didn't have enough ornaments. She got out some of her old scraps of cloth and sewed some ornaments and made a beautiful cloth star. She ran out of yellow cloth, so the longest point was made of scraps from her husband's old coat. When the kids came home, they saw the tree and danced around it. Alvin looked especially surprised.

"When does Santa come?" Michael, the youngest, asked.

"On Christmas Eve," Alvin said. That reminded him there was only two weeks until Christmas. He had to hurry. He looked at their lists and saw John had listed a pocketknife. He took out his pocketknife out of his box of precious things. His father gave it to him before he left to serve in the war. He didn't know if he could give it away, but just as he put it back in his box, John walked in.

"Could I use your pocketknife just for a little while?" he asked.

Alvin took it back out and gave it to John. Later that night, he saw John take it in his hands and just look longingly at it. Then he gave it back to Alvin. Alvin saw that look on John's face and knew that he would give it to him. Alvin asked his mother how to get Linda a doll for Christmas.

"I have some scraps I can use to make her a doll." His mother spent all night making that doll. Alvin couldn't sleep and saw a little bit of light glowing from a candle. The next day, Alvin was looking at little Michael's list. Alvin knew how much he wanted that little bear in the toy store, but it cost one whole dollar. Alvin took out his precious box and got out a dollar and put it in his pocket. When Alvin came home from the grocery store, he would buy it.

At the grocery store, Mr. Gearly asked Alvin what he wanted for Christmas.

"Nothing; I don't want anything," he said.

"Surely there must be something," Mr. Gearly said.

Mr. Gearly was a woodcarver in his spare time. He had some of his carvings for sale in his store. This month, he had a manger scene. More than once, Mr. Gearly caught Alvin staring at the manger scene and Baby Jesus. Then he knew what Alvin wanted for Christmas. It was the last day of the Christmas season, so Mr. Gearly gave Alvin a peppermint stick and let him go home early.

Alvin went to the toy store. The little brown bear was still sitting in the window. He picked it up and came to the counter. He was so hungry, the store had caramel apples, his favorites, and other chocolates. Just as he looked at the price, he saw the train. Peter had wanted a train for three years, ever since his best friend had gotten one for his birthday. When trains came through the little town, Peter would be wide-eyed and would stare at the thundering train. It cost three dollars. It sure was beautiful, though. He picked up the train instead of the caramel apples and got the furry chocolate brown bear out of the window. He had spent all the money his mother had given him. When he showed his mom the treasures, she told him they could probably make all the other things.

Gretchen wanted a picture of Santa Claus. Alvin wasn't a great drawer, but he could try. He had one charcoal pencil and got out an unused piece of paper, which was hard to come by. He started out with the eyes. He had no picture, so he thought about his dad's eyes. He had eyes that twinkled and rosy cheeks. When he came to the mouth, it was a little bit too small, but not bad for his age. Then came the bushy eyebrows, beard, and mustache. The only person he knew with a white mustache was Mr. Gearly, and when Alvin finished, he was impressed. It wasn't perfect, but for a twelve year old, it looked pretty good.

Finally, Anne wanted a book. She had just started to read, but the only book they had in the house was the Bible. Alvin had no money, and the only person he knew who had a book was his teacher. It was getting late, and it was cold and snowy outside, but he got on his worn-out coat and trudged through the snow to her house. He didn't know what he would say to her. He knocked on the door, and Mrs. Peters answered it.

"Come right in, Alvin," she said. "What are you doing here?"

"My sister wants a book for Christmas," Alvin said. "I don't have any money, and the only person I could think of that might have a spare book was you."

"Let's see what we can find," she said. She opened a closet full of books. "How old is your sister?" Mrs. Peters asked.

"About five," he said.

"Here's a great book with some pictures in it; she will love it."

Alvin took it home and gave it to his mother.

"Where did you get this?" she asked.

"From Mrs. Peters," Alvin said.

"Put in it with all of the other presents," his mom said.

Today was Christmas Eve. Alvin only had one peppermint stick left, so he broke it into small pieces and gave all of his siblings a piece. Then his mom said she was going to make some candy. That meant he was supposed to take the kids outside and around the town. He took them to Mr. Gearly's store, and he saw that he was in there. Alvin went inside and asked him what he was doing there on Christmas Eve night.

"Oh, doing some special orders," he said.

Alvin went back out to the front window and took one last glance at the beautiful manger scene. Mr. Gearly saw the look on Alvin's face and waited until Alvin was out of sight and took down the manger scene and wrapped it in the brightest wrapping paper he could find and tied a big red bow on the top.

When Alvin arrived home, he was excited, because tonight he could put the presents under the tree. That night, his mom got out Alvin's dad's Bible and read aloud the story of Christ's birth. Then the children got out their thin, worn stockings and hung them up. Then they went to bed. Alvin and his mother got out the candy and oranges from Mr. Gearly's package. Under the tree, they wrapped the presents in brown paper, because they had no wrapping paper. They wrapped Linda's doll, John's pocketknife, Michael's bear, Anne's book, Gretchen's picture, Peter's train, and Alvin had written a poem for his mother that he put under the tree for Christmas morning.

"I love you, Mom," he said.

"Love you, too," his mom said.

Alvin went to sleep, and Mr. Gearly stopped by.

"This is the manger scene that Alvin wanted," Mr. Gearly said,

"Oh, thank you so much," Alvin's mother said. "I didn't have any money left, and Alvin made all of these presents for his brothers and sisters."

"Good-night, Mr. Gearly," she said. "Merry Christmas."

She hurried and put Alvin's present under the tree and hung up Alvin's stocking with a special letter inside. Then she went to bed.

"Wake up! Wake up!" Michael said. Alvin woke up. He could smell Christmas sausages. He ran down the stairs, slipped the poem under the tree, and took down his stocking. In his stocking was an orange, candy, and a beautifully written letter. He hadn't thought he would get anything.

"Look, an orange," John shouted. Candy of every sort was in the stocking, especially his favorites: chocolate and caramel-dipped pretzels. Now, for the Santa presents. Linda opened hers first. It was the doll his mother had made. It was the most beautiful doll and had a red dress and long braided hair.

John opened his gift. It was the pocketknife. Michael opened his gift, and it was the little brown bear. Then Anne opened her book. She was so careful to not to ruffle the pages. Gretchen opened the Santa drawing, and she taped it against the wall. Peter opened his gift last, and when he saw the shiny train, he nearly collapsed with excitement.

Gretchen reached under the tree and grabbed another gift. It was for Alvin. He held it until Linda urged him to open it. He slowly unwrapped it and opened the box and saw the manger carvings from the store. Tears of joy ran down his cheeks and he hugged his mother until he remembered his gift to her. It was a poem.

CHRISTMAS

Christmas is a time of giving, loving, and sharing.
It doesn't matter what's under the tree; it's about caring.
The gift of love was given so long ago
That we have forgotten what the true meaning of Christmas is, so

Here's a reminder to help you out:
You cannot say Christmas without Christ.

He looked up at his mother, and she was crying. He didn't know why, but he knew he loved his family so much, and nothing else mattered.

Used by Permission of the Author.

A Christmas Snow Globe

ALISON R. DUNN

I grew up not knowing whether we were rich or poor. "Hey, Mom, does Dad make _____?" The amount never really mattered; I couldn't comprehend what you could buy with a thousand dollars vs. a million dollars. That was not my real question; I wanted to know if we were "rich." Rich, as in elementary school kid rich, rich like we could buy a fancy car or big boat if we wanted to.

I would throw out numbers to my mom, numbers I had heard at school that the kids said you were rich if you made more than that amount. For some reason, my parents never really answered my questions.

Some days, I thought we must be pretty poor, because when I asked for the newest toy or the latest pair of jeans, my parents always said, "No" or "You can use your own money." Some days, I thought we must be doing OK, mostly when we would drive through the run-down neighborhoods around town or see a family with not much in their shopping cart.

Looking back on it, I realize now that we were quite well-off compared to most of the kids at my school. However, my parents never flaunted it, they never bought us the newest or the best, and they never let us know how much they made or what was in their bank account. We never had to wonder if there was food to eat or if we would receive birthday presents. And we never had to worry about if Santa or Christmas would be coming to our house.

Every year, my parents came to us children and asked if we would be willing to give up some of our Christmas so someone else could have a Christmas. "Sub for Santa," they called it. During those young, Santa-believing years, we still figured Santa was going to show up at their house, but maybe we could bring a few presents their parents might not be able to afford. Once we got older, we understood.

Memories of those Christmases vary greatly. Some years, I remember excitedly picking presents that the kids we were giving to might like. Others, I don't remember at all. Sometimes

I remember accompanying my parents to run-down apartments and houses. I always felt proud of our accomplishments and our ability to give.

However, those were not the lessons my parents intended to teach us. They wanted us to learn to be grateful, to be compassionate, and to be more "Christ-like." And thanks to a young boy named Tom and a young girl named Jenny, I was taught the spirit of Christmas.

That year, as the oldest, I overheard a lot of "adult conversations" surrounding our Sub-for-Santa family. I heard whispers, such as:

"A young father, who recently lost his wife."

"The bishop says he might not accept it, but they sure could use the help."

"He agreed, but only if we just gave food and necessities."

"No toys."

"He wants his children to be there when we drop off the items."

Most years we bought clothes, winter coats, boots, toys, food, and items for a Christmas. Usually, these things were brought to the door, when the children were not home, with rolls of wrapping paper so the parents could be included in the Christmas present festivities.

This entire year was turning out a little bit different than the others.

"No toys."

"He wants his kids to see us?"

It seemed a little strange, but my parents tried to abide by the rules. There may have been a basketball or other game that was included as a "necessity."

The day came to deliver "Christmas." I remember pulling up to a small house and walking down the steps to a small basement apartment. Everything was neat and clean and there was a *huge* Christmas tree stuffed into the small living room. Looking at the size of that "tree," my immediate thought was, that is the biggest tree I have ever seen, and I wonder if they really needed presents from us, if they could afford such a big tree. Looking back on it, that Christmas tree was so large and so bushy, it may have been more of a bush than an actual tree. No store or Christmas tree lot sold trees like that.

But standing there next to the tree that had only a very few ornaments and a paper chain to decorate it, was a young boy and an even younger girl, with huge smiles on their faces. They were so excited to see us, and as we were soon to find out that their excitement had nothing to do with what we were bringing in all of those boxes and bags. It had nothing to do with the presents, the food, the "Christmas" that I thought we were bringing.

They already had "Christmas," and we didn't bring it; they carried it with them. It was evident in their smiles and in their eyes. Their excitement was because of what they had to give us. For before we could even say hello or present our gifts, they had lovingly presented my mother with a baby food jar, snow globe, and a small wooden plaque with a cut-out Christmas card glued to the front and the names Jenny and Tom signed on the front.

I wish each year that I helped in playing Santa that I carried that same excitement of Christmas in my eyes, and I know that I did not. The expressions I most carried with me ranged from bashful, proud, scared, and sometimes disgusted by the circumstances we found. But that Christmas, I was given a true gift of Christmas, a Christmas lesson. A lesson that taught me that giving has very little to do with the cost or niceness of the present; giving is a feeling, an excitement that is only present when giving true gifts of love and selfishness.

As I gaze on the small plaque that still takes a prominent spot in my mother's Christmas decorations each year, I remember those two small children and the lesson that giving is always better than receiving.

Used by Permission of the Author.

Two Christmas Phone Calls

DARRELL B. SONNTAG

I didn't think I was going to cry, until I heard the voice of my dad. It was Christmas Day, and I was seven months into my mission in Rome. I had arrived in Italy the end of July, and was now serving in the city of Cagliari, the largest city on the island of Sardinia. This was my first phone call home.

Once I heard the voice of my dad say hello on the other end of the phone call, I just lost it. All of my emotions came to the surface—a tangible love for my family, homesickness for being away from the---all coupled with the stress I was feeling as a missionary. I was struggling with my companion, I felt there was more we could do as missionaries, but as a junior companion, I didn't know what to do. I was still struggling to speak the language, I felt I was behind in learning the language compared to other missionaries, and I still hadn't memorized all the discussions yet (like my dad and brother, Dave, had done a few months into their missions).

I was embarrassed to tell them how the work was going, because in my eyes, it wasn't going. We didn't have any real investigators, and I don't think we had taught a real discussion in a long time or if at all as a companionship. The mission was not what I had envisioned it to be, and I wasn't having a great spiritual or missionary experience, and I felt that it was my own fault. I felt like I was disappointing my family.

I don't remember what was said on the rest of the phone call, but I remember feeling uplifted by the love of my family, and that gave me strength and courage to go on.

Fast-forward to next year's Christmas Day. On Christmas Eve (La Vigilia d'Natale), my companion and I were invited to have Christmas Eve with Tina Vutterielo, a recent convert to the church, who lived in an public housing block in an industrial section of Naples, with her

160

non-member husband, Salvatore, her three daughters (including her handicapped daughter Angela, who would affectionately pinch us), and extended family.

Tina joined the church at much sacrifice as the only member of her family. Salvatore was unemployed, and Tina supported the family from her job, but also took care of her family and generously fed us missionaries on a weekly basis. They made us feel part of the family (I remember cheating at the Napolitano Christmas bingo game so Angela would win.) I remember feeling so much love for her and her family and gratitude for the opportunity to be His missionary in Napoli at Christmas time.

I remember calling my family the next day, without crying at all! I remember being excited to tell them about a new investigator we had found, Mikail Potapov, a young Russian student living in Napoli, who we had just began teaching and was believing the lessons we taught to him. Teaching Mikail was the highlight of my mission—throwing his cigarettes in the garbage bin, going with him to meet his skateboarding friends—in his hope that they, too, would be able to feel "lo Spirito Santo" (The Holy Ghost). Within a month, by the end of January, I was able to baptize Mikail a member of the Church of Jesus Christ of Latter-day Saints.

My experience with the two Christmas Day phone calls and my experience teaching Mikail was a lesson on Christ's grace. I didn't direct our paths to meet on the street in the middle of Naples. I didn't send the Holy Ghost to feel his heart. I did not convert Mikail Potapov. The Lord did. Christ expects us to do our best. That's it. He makes up the difference in our many weaknesses. Sometimes things will be harder than we expected, sometimes they will take longer, but in the end, He is the Lord of the Harvest, and we will never be disappointed in serving Him.

Used by Permission of the Author.

Wise Men

STEPHANIE L. JENSEN (age 13)

Three men. Seeking peace, light, and strength. The first one named Alati. Alati took care of his mother until she died. Her death caused Alati such sadness. He wanted his mother to stay with him. Alati had difficulty understanding why the Lord allows sad things to happen to us. He wanted peace.

The second man, Bruni, had a stutter. Because of this, his friends and family rejected him and considered his condition a sign of unrighteousness. Bruni lived alone. He wondered why his own family would reject him. He felt abandoned by God, even though he tried to do what is right. Bruni desired light.

The third man, Catapus, had no leg below his right knee. As a child, he was teased. When he got older, the marriage arranger told him he wasn't worth arranging. No one would marry such a man. Catapus had a hard time finding work, but a sympathetic farmer felt sorry for him and paid him to clean animal stalls. Catapus was also confused; why would a loving God give him an imperfect leg? He wanted strength.

One afternoon, after Catapus finished cleaning the stalls, he saw Bruni. "Bruni," he said. "I haven't seen you for at least a week. How are you?"

"Not so well," Bruni said. "I have to go home to a dark house. I don't feel like going home."

"Well, don't," Catapus said. "Come over to my house. I'm sure Alati will be along soon. At least the three outcasts have some companionship."

Down the road came Catapus. As he stumbled down the road, he approached the two men with his curly and unwieldy brown hair.

"Let's go see Figel," Alati said. "We haven't seen him in ages."

Catapus looked at Alati, who had been in a constant bad mood since his mother died, and agreed. All three trudged up the sandy path, steadying Catapus. As they continued down the path, they passed aging olive trees in Figel's courtyard. They slowly stepped up to Figel's front door and knocked. They heard the hoarse voice of an old man, and a wrinkled face curved out from the door.

Figel was sort of a mystic in the neighborhood. He had a long white beard and gray hair, with a few dark hairs sprayed through. He had fluid eyes.

"Enter at once!" Figel said, herding them in with his hands. "I've been waiting for you. I have something to show you."

In Figel's mysterious, dusty dwelling, there were unusual books and manuscripts of all different colors and sizes. The house had all sorts of books spilled over every table, leftover remnants of food, and birds, dogs, and cats all over the room. Figel led the three to what he called the "thinking spot." It was a small room connected to the library and covered with pillows and lined with windows. Bruni helped Catapus sit down, and Alati almost tripped. Figel reached up on his tiptoes and pushed back a wooden slab, displaying a purple night sky.

"Incredible! Look at the strength of the light of those distant stars," sighed Catapus.

"I feel the light of the luminous stars," Bruni said.

"I sense the peace from their light and strength," Alati said.

"Now, a fortnight ago, I was in my thinking spot, and I noticed in the West a shooting star," Figel said. "Now, you may be questioning why I am so excited by a single star; it is because of the brightness and the position of this new star. The star has a different light I have never seen before. It is a star of all stars, a light of all lights. It beckons me."

They looked at the star. It overpowered the rest of the stars with its bright light. It almost looked like a planet, it was so bright.

After looking at the star for several minutes, Figel lit an oil lamp. The lamp illuminated half of Figel's wrinkled face.

"You must follow the new star," he said.

"What!" Alati said.

"Why must we?" said Catapus. "You know I can't walk."

"There will be sacrifices," Figel said. "I would go with you, but I know my old, broken body will not survive the long journey. The reward will be great. It is a journey for wise men."

"Where does the star lead?" Bruni asked.

"The prophets of old have long been foretelling the birth of a Savior of the world in Bethlehem of Judea. A new star shall arise to mark the birth of this Savior. This star must be followed. On this journey, you will discover the things you are seeking," Figel said. Figel was a lighthearted man, but when it came to religion, he was very serious. Figel had long been ready to seek the promised Messiah, but now he was sick and old.

Catapus thought about his life. He had little money, few friends, and his heart yearned for change. "I will go," Catapus said.

Bruni and Alati were humbled by the determination of a crippled man.

"I will go as well," Bruni said.

"I will take the journey and Figel with me," Alati said. "If we can make the journey, so can you. We will not abandon you. Come with us."

"Ah, you can see right through me," Figel said. "I was wishing you would say that."

The four men began to prepare for their long journey toward the star. Figel left his home to his nephew, taking only his most precious manuscripts of astronomy and religion for the journey. Bruni sold his humble dwelling, taking his friendly dog and some extra gold. Catapus sadly waved farewell to his animals, locked the door to his home, and took some frankincense that was given to him at his birth. Finally, Alati locked the door to his home and brought the last letter from his mother before she died. Attached to that letter was myrrh.

The four men bought camels and some travel gear and started out across the sandy desert. They moved slowly, stopping for the night, sleeping under the stars, and watching the new star.

The desert heat weakened Figel even more. He talked less and less and ate little at night.

One morning, Bruni woke and packed up the camp. He tried to waken Figel, but he would not open his eyes. Finally, Figel opened his eyes and spoke.

"I'm slowing you down," Figel said, turning his head away from Bruni. "You'll never make it if I continue with you. Leave me here."

Catapus refused. "No, I will take your camel, tie it behind mine, and I will hold you firmly and fan your face."

This took a lot of strength from Catapus. Figel had no strength, and Catapus had to grip him firmly. He constantly fanned and provided him with water. Catapus' arms got so tired at night he would collapse on top of his mats and not stir until the morning.

Alati would read to Figel out of his scriptures, words of peace and comfort. Alati knew how to care for the sick because of his mother. He would talk to Figel about the Messiah. Alati learned to have patience. There were nights when Alati had to stay up all night because Figel was distressed.

"What if I don't make it?" Figel would ask. "I have waited for this day all my life. I want to see the Messiah."

Bruni loved Figel and served the others as well. He gathered food for the dinners, supplied water, and gave his pillow and blanket to Figel, though the ground was hard and cold. He stayed up later and got up earlier than the rest of the camp to ward off thieves. He walked so that one of the camels could be free to carry the supplies for the journey.

The bright star came closer and closer. The travelers were only a week away from the walls of Bethlehem. One clear morning, Bruni awoke and got the camels ready, and he brought out dried figs and dates along with some dried bread. He woke up Catapus and then Alati. When he got to Figel, he knew something was wrong.

Figel had a peaceful look on his face, but he would not move, and his limbs were cold.

"Catapus! Alati! Figel hasn't made it through the night."

The other two rushed over to Figel's side.

"He's gone," Bruni said.

The three sadly buried Figel that afternoon, and the next day, they continued on their journey. When they reached Bethlehem, the star was glimmering above the town, and it was the brightest it had been so far. They continued in and followed the star, where it seemed to rest above a small cave dwelling near petrified sand dunes.

They entered into the little dwelling and saw a young woman holding a newborn baby and sitting beside a straw manger. A man sat next to her and each looked with amazement at the child. The baby was sleeping.

"We have come from the East to worship the promised Messiah," Alati said.

The woman nodded and beckoned them in.

They walked single file over the straw and into the room to see the baby. The baby looked like any other baby, but Bruni felt calm when the baby opened his eyes and looked at him. He felt that nothing else mattered.

Bruni pulled out some of the gold from his tattered robe. Catapus gave the mother sweet frankincense, and Alati brought the myrrh from his mother.

165

"Would you like to hold the child?" the mother asked, and she looked no more than fifteen years old. "It looks like you have come a long way to see him."

She picked up the baby and placed him in Catapus' arms. He felt the weightlessness of the child, a still, small voice whispered to him.

"By serving your friends, you have gained strength. You sought strength and found it when you helped others."

Catapus then placed the child in Alati's arms. He looked at the baby's calm face. Alati felt peace fill his soul. A voice whispered, "You have found peace. You have served me in your journey through serving your friend Figel. You have spoken the words that I placed into your heart. You found peace through speaking peace to others."

Alati passed the child finally to Bruni. As soon as he held the child swaddled in cloth, he felt the warmth of the baby. He heard a small voice saying, "You have helped your fellow men and have shown charity to others. This is the way to feel light and warmth. I am with you when you serve others."

Then Bruni placed the baby, who was now sleeping, back into the manger. The three men felt the presence of Figel. A gentle wind seemed to say, "It is a journey that only wise men take. I met the Savior before I expected. The father turned to the men and asked, "Have you men found what you were seeking?"

Used by Permission of the Author.

A Grandfather's Testimony

LaVON JONES

I would like to bear my testimony to the truthfulness of the gospel of Jesus Christ. Every day, I see things that convince me that there is a God in heaven, a great architect, and a great creator who has created this earth and all of the beauties in it. I think about the flowers, the trees, the crops, the bees, the hummingbirds, and the wind. I think of all the devices that are created by the God of Heaven to pollinize the flowers and the crops. You never see a rose turning out to be a sunflower or a gardenia to be some other kind of flower or a daisy crossing over to be a tulip. I don't know how these things are accomplished, but by whatever means, I see that the same pollination is achieved

The same process occurs with animals. The domestic animals are able to bring forth their offspring usually every twenty-eight to thirty days. The wild animals are designed to only bring forth their offspring in the spring of the year. Think of how the mother bear can go into hibernation, the cubs are born, and the mother gives the milk and nourishment to those cubs all during hibernation. All of those things just don't happen.

I think about the youngest granddaughter we have at this time, little Heather, and when we were invited down on that fast Sunday for her name and blessing. We held that sweet little girl in our arms and I looked at her little fingernails, the size of a match head, no bigger, and how all parts of her body were so perfect, as are all of our bodies. It is such a blessing and a comfort for me to know that there is a God of heaven who has organized and created all of these things for our good and our benefit. The human life is so perfect, even though some cells and parts of the body never develop for some infants. The Lord doesn't come back to correct those things; he organized all those things in the beginning. Everything that man makes or is able to design or build will either wear out, fail, fall apart, or will fail to function. The creations of God go on forever.

Think of the sun, the moon, the stars, and the rotations of the heavens. How the Big and Little Dipper rotate around the North Star and how the Dipper and the two stars always point to the North Star. These are wonders in heaven! There is a plan that is organized to keep all these things in order. So I know that there is a God in heaven who directs and who has created this earth through His Son, Jesus Christ. These things are here for our good and for our enjoyment. I know that the way has been opened up.

The Savior of the world gave his life as a sacrifice for us that we might be able to be resurrected and return back to the presence of the Father. We can go on to our exaltation if we but serve him, keep his commandments, and try to live by the things that the great Savior of the world taught us, the man from Galilee. I know that He is the son of Mary and the Son of God. I know that He is the God of this earth. I know that He lived and died and was crucified for us. I know that these things are all in the great, organized plan in the creation of this earth for the fulfillment for our joy and happiness and our exaltation. I know that God lives and that Jesus Christ is the Savior of the world, and I bear this witness and testimony to you.

References

REFERENCES FOR PARTS 1, 2, & 3

PREFACE

- Thomas S. Monson, "Because He Came," *Ensign*, Christmas Devotional 2011, lds.org. © By Intellectual Reserve, Inc.

PART ONE

- Jeffrey R. Holland, "Without Ribbons and Bows," *New Era,* December 1994, lds.org. © By Intellectual Reserve, Inc.

PART TWO

- Rosemary Wixom, "What Happened Next?" Christmas Devotional 2013, lds.org/broadcasts. © By Intellectual Reserve, Inc.

PART THREE

- Thomas S. Monson, "In Search of the Christmas Spirit," *Ensign,* December 1987, lds.org.© By Intellectual Reserve, Inc.

REFERENCES--NATIVITY-CENTERED BOOKS

Music: *Children's Songbook of the Church of Jesus Christ of Latter-day Saints*. Salt Lake City: The Church of Jesus Christ of Latter-Day Saints, 2000.

All books and stories are listed by title for ease in finding references. The annotations allow for easily substituting different books or stories.

BOOKS

- *Amahl and the Night Visitors*, Gian Carlo Menotti, illustrated by Michele Lemieux. New York: William Morrow Company, Inc. 1986.
  » Story of a poor, crippled shepherd boy who goes with the three kings to give his own gift to the Christ Child. (school age and older)
- *An Orange for Frankie*, Patricia Polacco. New York: Philomel Books, 2004.
  » George shows his family the true meaning of Christmas when he gives something he cherishes to someone who needs it more. His family shows him the same love through their generosity. (school age and older)
- *Angela and the Baby Jesus*, Frank McCourt, illustrated by Raul Colon, New York: Simon & Schuster Books for Young Readers, 2007.
  » Angela worries about the Baby Jesus on display in the church yard being cold as he lies in a manger. She literally takes matters into her own hands as she tries to care for Baby Jesus. (school age and older)
- *Away in a Manger*, Mike Jaroszko, St. Louis: Concordia Publishing House, 2009.
  » This book invites the reader to come to the stable and see the Christ Child and feel the peace and glory of the night He was born.
- *The Boy of the Bells*, Carly Simon, illustrated by Margot Datz, New York: Doubleday, 1990.
  » Grandfather asks Ben to be the bell ringer on Christmas Eve. Ben devises a plan to help his sister, Miranda, speak again.

- *Boxes for Katje*, Candace Fleming, illustrated by Stacey Dressen-McQueen, New York: Melanie Kroups Books, 2003.
  - » In the aftermath of World War II, Katje receives a care package from Rosie in America. Katje shares what she receives with others and finds a gift to send to Rosie. (school age and older)
- *The Candymaker's Gift*, David and Helen Haidle, Tulsa, Oklahoma, Honor Books, 1996.
  - » A candymaker decides to make a special treat that will tell the story of Jesus's birth and remind the children of Christ.
- *The Carpenter's Gift*, David Rubel, illustrated by Jim LaMarche. New York: Random House Children's Books, 2011.
  - » Henry assists his unemployed father in cutting spruce trees and taking them to New York City to sell for Christmas trees. They give the trees they can't sell to the construction workers who show up on Christmas Day with enough lumber to build Henry's family a simple home. (school age and older)
- *Christmas Day in the Morning*, Pearl S. Buck, illustrated by Mark Buehner, New York: Harper Collins Publishers, 1988.
  - » Rob wants to give his father a special gift for Christmas. He decides the perfect gift would be giving his dad a day off from milking the cows. (school age and older)
- *Christmas for a Dollar*, Gale Sears, illustrated by Ben Sowards, American Fork, Utah. Covenant Communications, 2009.
  - » A recent widower surprises his children with a dollar in coins for them to use to make or buy gifts for each other for Christmas. This book helps children see the joy in creating gifts for others. (school age)
  - » Also, available on DVD. (approximately 19 minutes)
- *Christmas Farms*, Mary Lyn Ray, illustrated by Barry Root, Boston: HMH Books for Young Readers, 2013.
  - » Wilma and Parker, her five-year-old neighbor, plant balsam seedlings. They continue to nurture and expand their Christmas tree farm.

- *The Christmas Miracle of Jonathan Toomey,* Susan Wojciechowski, illustrated by PJ Lynch, Cambridge, Massachusetts. Candlewick Press, 1995.
  - » Jonathan Toomey is a master woodcarver and has become sad and isolated since the death of his wife and child. As he carves a Nativity for a widow and her son, he learns to love again. (school age and older)
- *The Christmas Star,* Marcus Pfister, New York: North-South Books, 1993.
  - » The stars flowed together and merged into a huge star, which guided the shepherds, three kings, and the animals to a perfect place to welcome the Holy Child. (preschool and school age)
- *Christmas Tapestry,* Patricia Polacco, New York: Philomel Books, 2002.
  - » Jonathan and his father find a tapestry to cover the damaged wall of the church. The tapestry weaves a beautiful Christmas miracle. (school age and older)
- *The Christmas Train,* Thomas S. Monson, illustrated by Dan Burr, Salt Lake City: Shadow Mountain, 2012.
  - » Based on an experience Thomas S. Monson had as a young boy when he wanted a train car from a train set his mom was giving to a neighbor boy.
- *The Crippled Lamb,* Max Lucado, illustrated by Fabian Negrin, Nashville: Thomas Nelson, Inc. 1998.
  - » Joshua is a lamb who has a crippled leg and often feels left out. On the night Jesus is born, Joshua discovers that although he is different, he can give Baby Jesus a gift. (preschool and school age)
- *Father and Son, Nativity Story,* Gerda Marie Scheidl, illustrated by Marcus Pfister, New York: North-South Books, Henry Holt and Company, 2006.
  - » This story, narrated by Joseph, seeks to answer his question: "How do I raise the baby who created the earth and has given me everything?" (school age)
- *The First Christmas, The King James Version,* illustrated by Jan Pienkowski. New York: Alfred A. Knopf, 1984.
  - » The story of Jesus's birth quoted from Luke and Matthew is beautifully illustrated with silhouettes. (all ages)
- *The First Noel,* illustrated by Jody Wheeler, Nashville: Ideal Publications, 2010.
  - » Gives the history of "The First Noel" and the music and lyrics with illustrations.

- *Four Candles for Simeon*, Gerda Marie Scheidl, illustrated by Marcus Pfister, New York: North-South Books, Henry Holt and Company, 1987.
  - » Simeon, a young shepherd boy, is given four candles to search for a lost lamb. On his way, he meets people who need light as well. In the end, he discovers the true source of light. (school age)
- *The Fourth Wise Man*, based on the story by Henry Van Dyke, retold by Susan Summers, illustrated by Jackie Morris, New York: Dial Books for Young Readers, 1998.
  - » The story of Artaban, the fourth wise man who was scheduled to meet the other three wise men but chooses to serve others with the gifts he has brought for the king. (school age and older)
- *The Friendly Beasts: An Old English Christmas Carol*, illustrated by Tomie dePaola, New York: Penguin Putnam Books for Young Readers, 1981.
  - » This old English carol lets the animals tell the gifts they give to Baby Jesus. (pre-school to school age)
- *Gifts of the Heart*, Patricia Polacco, New York: G. P. Putman's Sons, 2013.
  - » On Trisha and Richie's last Christmas on the farm, they learn from their new housekeeper, Kay Lamity, about how to give unforgettable gifts from the heart.
- *The Gift of the Magi*, O. Henry, illustrated by Lisbeth Zwerger, London: North-South Books, 1982.
  - » Famous short story about a young couple willing to sacrifice their treasures for each other. This edition has beautiful Old World illustrations. (school age and older)
- *The Gingerbread Doll*, Susan Tews, illustrated by Megan Lloyd, New York: Clarion Books, 1993.
  - » Depression-era story about a mother who makes a gingerbread doll for her daughter as a substitute for the porcelain doll she wanted. (school age)
- *Good King Wenceslas*, as read by Jane Seymour, illustrated by Omar Rayyan, Salt Lake City, Shadow Mountain. 2012.
  - » Includes a DVD of the story read with the Mormon Tabernacle Choir and the Orchestra at Temple Square.

REFERENCES

- *Humphrey's First Christmas*, Carol Heyer, Nashville: Ideal Children's Books, 2007.
  - » A proud camel named Humphrey seeks to regain his favorite blanket while following a star to Bethlehem. But when he meets Baby Jesus, he is overcome with love and willingly gives up his treasured blanket to the true Master. (preschool to school age)
- *Jacob's Gift*, Max Lucado, illustrated by Robert Hunt, Nashville: Thomas Nelson, Inc. 1998.
  - » The story of Jacob, an apprentice carpenter who gives away his prize feed trough so Baby Jesus will have a comfortable place to sleep. Joseph's kind nature is shown in how he treats Jacob. (school age and older)
- *The Last Straw*, Fredrick H. Thury, illustrated by Vlasta van Kampen, Watertown, Massachusetts. Charlesbridge Publishing, 1998.
  - » Hoshmakaka, a proud camel, is chosen to carry the wise men's gifts to the Christ Child. Along the way, he agrees to carry numerous other gifts, which makes his burden heavy. (school age and older)
- *Legend of the Poinsettia*, Tomie dePaola, New York: Puffin, 1997.
  - » Tells the Mexican legend of the poinsettia and how a girl's gift to the Christ Child turns from something simple to something grand.
- *The Little Donkey*, Gerds Marie Scheidl, illustrated by Bernadette Watts, New York: North-South Books, 1988.
  - » A little donkey longed to go to Bethlehem to visit the baby born to be a king, and fighting his fears, he finally arrives to honor the Christ Child. (preschool to school age)
- *The Little Fir Tree*, Margaret Wise Brown, illustrated by Jim Lamarche, New York: Harper Collins Publishers, 2005
  - » A small fir tree, that lives alone in the forest, is delighted when the father of a bed-ridden boy comes and takes the tree home.
- *The Little One*, Pamela C. Reid, American Fork, Utah. Covenant Communications, 2010.
  - » Little One, a donkey, worries that he will never be big or strong enough. He learns that everyone has a unique purpose. (preschool to school age)
  - » Also available on DVD

- *The Little Shepherd's Christmas*, Carol Heyer, Nashville: Ideals Children's Books, 2011.
  - » Reuel's first night to help his brothers tend the sheep turns out to be the most important night of all. (school age)
- *The Little Shepherd Girl*, Juliann Henry, illustrated by Jim Madsen, Colorado Springs, Colorado. David C. Cook, 2007.
  - » Sarah pleads with her father until he agrees to let her tend the sheep with her cousins. When the star appears and the angels declare the birth of the Christ Child, Sarah takes her sheep and goes in search of Baby Jesus. (school age)
- *The Man of the House at Huffington Row*, Mary Brigid Barrett, San Diego, California. Gulliver Books, 1998.
  - » Francis O'Shea is determined to cheer up his sister, Katherine, with a special surprise on Christmas morning. He and Katherine both awake to a snowy Christmas miracle. (school age and older)
- *The Mansion 100th Anniversary Edition*, Henry Van Dyke, illustrated by Dan Burr, Salt Lake City, Utah. Shadow Mountain Publishing, 2011.
  - » In a dream, a wealthy man is shown that his prestigious gifts given to impress others do not have eternal rewards. Anniversary edition includes an abridged version suitable for children. (school age or older)
- *The Nativity*, artwork by J. Kirk Richards, Salt Lake City: Shadow Mountain, 2012.
  - » Beautiful artwork illustrating the text taken from the King James Version of the Holy Bible and the passages pertaining to the birth of Jesus Christ.
- *The Nativity Mary Remembers*, Laurie Knowlton, illustrated by Kasi Kubiak, Honesdale, Pennsylvania. Boyds Mills Press, 1998. (currently out-of-print)
  - » Jesus's mother, Mary, recalls what it was like to be the mother of Jesus. (school age)
- *Penny's Christmas Jar Miracle*, Jason F. Wright, illustrated by Ben Sowards, Salt Lake City, Utah, Shadow Mountain, 2009.
  - » This year it is Penny's turn to choose whom they will give the coins they had collected all year in their Christmas jar. She chooses to hold a neighborhood party for Mr. Charlie, an ailing, elderly widower.

- *Mr. Willowby's Christmas Tree,* Robert Berry. New York: Doubleday Book for Young Readers, 2000.
  - » A rhyming story of how Mr. Willowby's large Christmas tree is shared with other people and animals to bring Christmas joy to everyone. (preschool to school age)
- *Room for a Little One, a Christmas Tale,* Martin Waddell, illustrated by Jason Cockcroft, New York: Margaret K. McElderry Books, 2004.
  - » A tired donkey brings Mary into a stable, where they are welcomed by the other animals. (preschool)
- *Santa's Favorite Story, Santa Tells the Story of the First Christmas,* Hisako Aoki, illustrated by Ivan Gantschev. New York: Simon & Schuster Books of Young Readers, 1982.
  - » This story has Santa explaining to the animals that we celebrate Christ at Christmas, not Santa. (preschool to school age)
- *The Scallop Christmas,* Jane Freeberg, illustrated by Astrid Sheckels. Yarmouth, Maine: Islandport Press, 2009.
  - » Tender story about a family that takes advantage of an abundant harvest of scallops to work together to earn extra money for a Christmas surprise.
- *Shoemaker Martin,* based on a story by Leo Tolstoy, illustrated by Bernadette Watts. New York: North-South Books, 1986.
  - » One night, Martin, the shoemaker, was promised he could welcome the Savior to his home. The next day, he waits for the Savior to come while inviting those in need into his home. At the end of the day, Martin realizes the Savior was with him all along. (school age and older)
- *A Small Miracle,* Peter Collington, New York: Alfred A. Knopf, 1997.
  - » A wordless book about an old woman who uses her last resources to help repair the vandalism to her village church. In the end, she receives aid from those she helped. (school age and older)
- *The Sparkle Box,* Jill Hardie, illustrated by Christine Kornacki, Nashville, Tennessee, Ideals Children's Books, 2012.
  - » Sam learns about the true meaning of Christmas from a sparkling silver box that his parents promise they can open together when they have filled the box by giving to people in need.

- *The Storybook Set and Advent Calendar*, retold by Mary Packard, illustrated by Carolyn Croll, New York: Workman Publishing, 2008.
  - » An Advent calendar with twenty-four small books, telling the story of the birth of Jesus, each with a different character or event.
- *The Story of Christmas, King James Bible*, illustrated by Pamela Dalston, San Francisco: Handprint Books, 2011.
  - » The story of Jesus's birth directly from The *King James Bible* beginning with the angel Gabriel appearing to Mary. Illustrations compliment the story of the birth of Christ. (all ages)
- *The Tale of the Three Trees: A Traditional Folktale*, retold by Angela Elwell Hunt, illustrated by Tim Jonke, Batavia, Illinois. Lion Publishing, 1989.
  - » Three trees, all with great dreams, participate in Christ's life and find joy in easing his burdens. (school age and older)
- *There Was No Snow on Christmas Eve*, Pam Munoz Ryan, illustrated by Dennis Nolan. New York: Hyperion Books for Children, 2005. (currently out-of-print)
  - » This book contrasts the story of the Nativity in Bethlehem with the snow now associated with Christmas. Beautiful illustrations of Mary as the young, loving mother of Jesus. (preschool to school age)
- *This Is the Stable*, Cynthia Cotton, illustrated by Delana Bettoli, New York: Henry Holt and Company, 2006.
  - » A rhyming Nativity story with repetition that is perfect for young children. (preschool and school age)
- *We Three Kings*, illustrated by Gennady Spirin. New York: Atheneum Books for Young Readers, 2006.
  - » The Christmas carol, *We Three Kings*, accompanied with pictures. It shows the three kings following the star and presenting their gifts to Jesus. (all ages)
- *Why Christmas Trees Aren't Perfect*, Richard H. Schneider, illustrated by Elizabeth J. Miles. Nashville: Abingdon Press, 1988.
  - » Small Pine dreams of being the perfect Christmas tree but offers protection and nourishment to the animals of the forest at the expense of her beauty. She

learns that sharing, and not appearances, creates true beauty. (preschool to school age)

- *The Year of the Perfect Christmas Tree*, Gloria Houston, illustrated by Barbara Cooney, New York: Dial Books for Young Readers, 1988.
  » Ruthie is chosen to be the angel in the church Nativity program. Even though the family has no money, Ruthie's mother teaches her the true meaning of Christmas through love and sacrifice. (school age and older)

REFERENCES--NATIVITY-CENTERED CHRISTMAS STORIES

- "The Christmas Basket," Kate Strongin, *The Friend*, December 2009, lds.org
  » Story of how Katie and her family help another family at Christmas.
- "Christmas at the Hospital," Katy Johnson Gale, *The Friend*, December 2012, lds.org.
  » After a long hospital stay, Stacy is allowed to go home, but she wants to give all of her friends in the hospital a Christmas gift.
- "Christmas Eve Drop Off," Lisa Harvey, *The Friend*, December 2010, lds.org
  » Melissa wants to give her Christmas gifts away to a girl at school. Her family agrees, and they make special Christmas surprises for the girl and her family.
- "A Christmas Horse," Jeanne W. Pittman, *Ensign*, December, 1980, lds.org.
  » Nancy dreams of a horse for Christmas. Family circumstances change, and she discovers how to find true joy by sharing.
- "A Christmas Prayer," Peggy Schonken, *The Friend*, December 2012, lds.org.
  » When Peggy's family receives much needed food for their Christmas dinner, Peggy learns that Heavenly Father hears and answers prayers.
- "Doll Brings Lesson on Christmas," Adrianna Cabello, *Deseret News*, December 22, 2010, Salt Lake City, Utah. © Deseret News Publishing Company, reprinted courtesy of Deseret News Publishing Company.
  » Two sisters receive dolls for Christmas. When the younger sister breaks her doll, her older sister gives her prized doll to replace the one that was broken.
- "The Empty Box," Anonymous Original source unknown.
  » Classic story of a boy who makes a special box for his teacher and fills it with invisible love.
- "The Gift," Monica C. Webster, *The Friend*, December 2011, lds.org.
  » Isak gives his family a special gift for Christmas that reminds everyone of the gift Christ gave.

- "A Gift of the Heart," Norman Vincent Peale, *Readers Digest*, January 1968. Copyright Readers Digest Association.
  » Also found in various sites online and in print.
  » A maid honors the wealthy family she works for by purchasing a baby gift for a poor family in need.
- "Gloves for a Shepherd," Sara K., age twelve, *The Friend*, December 2013, lds.org.
  » A boy gives one pair of his gloves to the boy who was acting as a shepherd in a Nativity scene.
- "A Helping Angel," Mary Joanne Steck, *The Friend*, December 2013, lds.org.
  » Molly makes a friend when she helps Julia overcome her stage fright by going out onto the stage and helping her sing.
- "The Lights of Christmas," Hilary M. Hendricks, *The Friend*, December 2011, lds.org.
  » Jackson and his family learn the joys of helping others at Christmas.
- "The Littlest Camel," *The Littlest Camel and other Christmas Stories*, Bob Hartman, illustrated by Brett Hudson, Oxford: Lion Children's Book, 2004.
  » Little camel's struggles to keep up with his mother while the caravan travels to visit the Christ Child.
- "The Missing Egg," George Sterling Spencer, *The Friend*, December 2009, lds.org.
  » An eight-year-old boy wants to collect twelve eggs to give his mother for Christmas, and on Christmas morning he is still one egg short.
- "My Gift to Jesus," Rachel Lynn Bauer, *The Friend*, December 2012, lds.org.
  » A sister decides to give Jesus the gift of being nice to her younger sister.
- "Sharing Christmas," Annie Beer, *The Friend*, December 2011, lds.org
  » By giving, Sarah learns she can be like Jesus.
- "Straw for the Manger," Jacob F. Frandsin, *The Friend*, December 2010, lds.org.
  » Michael learns to give a gift to the Savior by placing a piece of straw in a manger each time he does a kind deed.
- "Tire Tracks and Twinkle Lights," Willis Rittner, *The Friend*, December 2009 lds.org.
  » Christy and her mom get stuck in the snow while they are out driving around looking at Christmas lights. Christy prays for someone to help them get home.

- "Two Dimes and a Nickel," Richard A. Robb, *Ensign*, December 1986, lds.org.
  - » Story of a young boy who gives his two dimes and a nickel to the bishop so the bishop could help his three friends like his dad was helping their mother.
- "Warming Up to the Lindsays," Marjorie A. Havens, *The Friend*, December 2013, lds.org.
  - » Karen changes her mind about the Lindsays, when Matthew Lindsay carries her home after her feet become soaked and her boots fill with cold water while they are cutting down a Christmas tree.
- "When Jesus Was a Child," Michelle Garrett, *The Friend*, December, 2013, lds.org.
  - » An explanation of what life was like for Jesus as a child.

REFERENCES--YOUNGER CHILDREN'S BOOKS
*INDICATES BOARD BOOK

- *The Animals' Christmas Eve, a Little Golden Book*, Racine, Wisconsin. Western Publishing Company. 1972.
  - » The animals in a barn all help tell the story of Christ's birth using numbers one to twelve.
- **Baby Jesus Is Born*, Val Chadwick Bagley, illustrated by Amy Mullins, American Fork, Utah. Covenant Communications, 2011.
  - » A board book shaped like a stable, tells the story of the birth of Baby Jesus with rhymes and simple illustrations.
- **The Christmas Star*, Barbara Shook Hazen, illustrated by Lucy Barnard, Bath, UK. Reader's Digest Children's Books, 2006.
  - » Simple retelling of the Christmas story, with a battery-operated star young children push to illuminate the story. (preschool)
- *A Christmas Goodnight*, Nola Buck, illustrated by Sarah Jane Wright, New York: Harper Collins, 2011.
  - » Wonderful introduction to the Nativity for very young children.
- **Christmas in the Manger*, Nola Buck, illustrated by Felicia Bond, New York: Harper Festival, 1994.
  - » One-page description of each person or animal present at the first Christmas, simply told.
- *Hurry! Hurry! Have You Heard?* Laura Krauss Melmed, illustrated by Jane Dyer, San Francisco: Chronicle Books, 2008.
  - » Lyric-verse book illustrated in soft watercolor drawings about sheep and other animals of the field and forest that come to see the Christ Child. Young children will recognize the familiar animals.

- *Joy to the World: A Sing-Along Christmas Pageant*, Nashville: Ideal Publications, 2010.
  » The song "Joy to the World" plays while the story is told of a Christmas pageant.
- *O Little Town of Bethlehem, A Pageant of Lights*, Nashville: Ideal Publications, 2010.
  » Listen to the Christmas carol while reading the story of the birth of Christ.
- *Silent Night, A Pageant of Light,* Nashville: Ideals Publications, 2006
  » When you open the first page, the song "Silent Night" plays, and a "halo" of light surrounds Baby Jesus as the book retells of the birth of Christ.
- *The Story of Christmas*, Patricia A. Pingry, illustrated by Rebecca Thornburgh, Nashville: Ideals Publications, 2010.
  » The story of the birth of Baby Jesus and how it relates to the gifts we give and receive at Christmas.

REFERENCES--TEEN/YOUNG ADULT STORIES AND BOOKS

- "A Surprise Visitor," Erin Parsons, *Christmas I remember best*, Salt Lake City, 1983, ©Deseret News Publishing Company, reprinted courtesy of Deseret News Publishing Company.
- "The Christmas Scout," Anonymous.
- "Where Are You, Christmas?" lyrics written by James Horner, Will Jennings, and Mariah Carey.
- "The Candy Bomber," Babzanne Park, *New Era*, December 1977, lds.org.
- *Candy Bomber: The Story of the Berlin Airlift's "Chocolate Pilot,"* Michael O. Tunnell, Watertown, Massachusetts: Charlesbridge Publishing, 2010.
- *Home for the Holidays*, (DVD/CD) live recording of the 2013 Mormon Tabernacle Choir Christmas Concert, 2012, Salt Lake City, Deseret Book 2013.
- *Christmas from Heaven: The True Story of the Candy Bomber*, Tom Brokaw, illustrated by Robert T. Barrett, Salt Lake City, Shadow Mountain, 2013.
- "The Whipping," Anonymous.
- "An Exchange of Gifts," Diane Rayner, is reproduced with permission from *Guideposts*, Guideposts.org. Copyright ©1983 by Guideposts. All rights reserved.
- "Maybe Christmas Doesn't Come from a Store," Jeffrey R. Holland, *Ensign*, December 1977, lds.org.
- *How the Grinch Stole Christmas*, New York, Random House, 1957.
- "To My Big Brother, Danny, Who I Love a Lot," *Others*, Blaine M. Yorgason and Brenton G. Yorgason, Salt Lake City: Bookcraft, 1976. Permission granted by Blaine Yorgason.
- "Once in a Lifetime Christmas," Will Wright. Available to print from sources online.
- "A Handmade Ornament," Stephanie L. Jensen. Permission granted by author.
- "The Good and Grateful Receiver," Dieter F. Uchtdorf, Christmas Devotional 2012, lds.org/broadcasts.

- "One Solitary Life," poem, Dr. James Allan Francis, 1926. Available on various online sites.
- "The Living Christ: The Testimony of the Apostles," Salt Lake City: The Church of Jesus Christ of Latter-day Saints, January 1, 2000.
- "Doll Brings Lesson on Christmas," Adrianna Cabello, *Deseret News*, December 22, 2010, Salt Lake City. © Deseret News Publishing Company, reprinted courtesy of Deseret News Publishing Company.
- *The Year of the Perfect Christmas Tree*, Gloria Houston, illustrated by Barbara Cooney, New York: Dial Books for Young Readers, 1988.
- "Hard Times," Janet Anderson Hurren, *Classic Christmas: True Stories of Holiday Cheer and Goodwill*. Edited, Helen Szymanski, Avon, Massachusetts: Adams Media, 2006.
- "A Gift for Louise," Pearl B. Mason, *Christmas I remember best*, Salt Lake City, 1983, © Deseret News Publishing Company, reprinted courtesy of Deseret News Publishing Company.

REFERENCES--ADULT VERSION-- STORIES AND BOOKS

- "I Knew You Would Come," Elizabeth King English is reproduced with permission from *Guideposts*, Guideposts.org. Copyright ©1983 by Guideposts. All rights reserved.
- "Waiting on the Road to Damascus," Dieter F. Uchtdorf, *Ensign*, May 2011, lds.org.
- "If You're Missing Baby Jesus," Jean Gietzen, illustrated by Lila Rose Kennedy, Colorado Springs, Colorado: Blue Cottage Gifts, division of Multnomah Books, 2001.
- "The Search for Jesus," Thomas S. Monson, *Ensign*, December 1990, lds.org.
- "What Shall I Do Then with Jesus Which Is Called Christ?" Gordon B. Hinckley, *Ensign,* December 1983, lds.org
- "Handful of Pennies," Ella Birdie Jamison, as told to Norma Favor, Permission granted by Norma Favor.
- "Think to Thank," Thomas S. Monson, *Ensign*, November 1998, lds.org.
- "The Legend of the Christmas Apple," Ruth Sawyer
- "The Gifts of Christmas," Thomas S. Monson, *Ensign*, December 2003, lds.org.
- "A Gift for a Stranger," Donavene Jaycox, *Ensign*, December 1998, lds.org.
- "Christmas Gifts, Christmas Blessings," Thomas S. Monson, *Ensign*, 1995, lds.org.
- "Jesus the Christ-Our Prince of Peace," Russell M. Nelson, Christmas Devotional 2013, lds.org/broadcasts.
- *Christmas Prayer*, Rian B. Anderson, American Fork, Utah: Covenant Communications, 2001.
- "The Perfect Gift," Henry B. Eyring, Christmas devotional, 2012. lds.org/broadcasts
- "Boxes Full of Love," Hope M. Williams, *Christmas I remember best*, Salt Lake City, 1983, © Deseret News Publishing Company, reprinted Courtesy of Deseret News Publishing Compamy.

- "A Christmas Dress for Ellen," Thomas S. Monson, illustrated by Ben Sowards, Salt Lake City: Shadow Mountain, 1998.
- *A Christmas Dress for Ellen*, Thomas S. Monson, Salt Lake City: Bookcraft, 1989. (booklet)
- *Angela and the Baby Jesus*, Frank McCourt, illustrated by Raul Colon, New York: Simon & Schuster Books for Young Readers, 2007.
- "Christmas Comfort," Jeffrey R. Holland, December 1, 1998, video.byui.edu/media.
- "Silent Night, Holy Night," Joseph B. Wirthlin, Salt Lake City, *Church News*, Saturday, November 29, 2008, Deseret News Publishing Company.
- "Come, Let Us Adore Him," Patrick Kearon, *Ensign*, December 2011, 30.
- "Bethann's Christmas Prayer," Marilyn Morgan Helleberg. Reprinted with permission from her husband, Robert King.
- "Angels, Once in a While," Barb Irwin, *Chicken Soup for the Singles Soul* by Jack Canfield, Mark Victor Hansen, Jennifer Read Hawthorne, and Marci Shimoff. Copyright 2012 by Chicken Soup for the Soul Publishing, LLC.
- "The Good and Grateful Receiver," Dieter F. Uchtdorf, Christmas Devotional 2012, lds.org/broadcasts.
- "What Happened Next?" Rosemary Wixom, Christmas Devotional 2013, lds.org/broadcasts.
- *The Scallop Christmas*, Jane Freeberg, illustrated by Astrid Sheckels: Yarmouth, Maine: Islandport Press, 2009.
- "What Shall I Do Then with Jesus Which Is Called Christ?," Gordon B. Hinckley, *Ensign*, December 1983, lds.org
- *Christmas Day in the Morning*, Pearl S. Buck, illustrated by Mark Buehner, New York: Harper Collins Publishers, 1988.
- *The Light of Thy Childhood Again*, Boyd K. Packer, Salt Lake City: Deseret Book, 1997.
- "Maybe Christmas Doesn't Come from a Store," Jeffrey R. Holland, *Ensign*, December 1977, lds.org © By Intellectual Reserve, Inc.

REFERENCES--STORIES OF THE SAVIOR'S LIFE

- Ezra Taft Benson, "The Savior's Visit to America," *Ensign*, May 1987, lds.org
- Ruth Cosby, "Cameron's Picture," *Ensign*, September 1994, lds.org.
- James E. Faust, "Five Loaves and Two Fishes," *Ensign*, May 1994, lds.org.
- Camille Fronk, "The Woman at the Well," *Arise and Shine Forth: Talks from the 2000 Women's Conference,* Bookshelf eBook, Salt Lake City: Deseret Book, 2000. Also found online at http://ce.byu.edu/cw/womensconference/pdf/archive/2000/fronk_camille.pdf
- Jeffrey R. Holland, "A High Priest of Things to Come," *Ensign*, October 1999, lds.org.
- Jeffrey R. Holland, "He Loved Them Until the End," *Ensign*, October 1989, lds.org.
- Jeffrey R. Holland, "None Were with Him," *Ensign*, May 2009, lds.org.
- Howard W. Hunter, "The Reason in the Harbor of Peace," *Ensign*, November 1992, lds.org.
- Eric Huntsman, "Reflections on the Savior's Last Week," *Ensign*, April 2009, lds.org.
- Neil A. Maxwell, "Overcome—Even as I also Overcame," *Ensign*, May 1987, lds.org.
- Thomas S. Monson, "Because He Came," Christmas Devotional, December 2011, lds.org/broadcasts.
- Thomas S. Monson, "For I Was Blind, but Now I See," *Ensign*, April 1999, lds.org.
- Thomas S. Monson, "The Divine Gift of Gratitude," *Ensign*, November 2010, lds.org.
- Thomas S. Monson, "He Is Risen," *Ensign*, May 2010, lds.org
- Thomas S. Monson, "Mercy—The Divine Gift," *Ensign*, May 1995, lds.org.
- Thomas S. Monson, "Teach the Children," *Ensign*, November 1997, lds.org.
- Thomas S. Monson, "With Hand and Heart," *Ensign*, October 1971, lds.org.
- Dallin H. Oaks, "Followers of Christ," *Ensign*, May 2013, lds.org.
- Bonnie D. Parkin, "Choosing Charity: That Good Part," *Ensign*, November 2003, lds.org

- Linda Reeves, "The Lord Has Not Forgotten You," *Ensign*, November 2012, lds.org.
- N. Eldon Tanner, "Christ in America," *Ensign*, May 1976, lds.org
- Joseph B. Wirthlin, "The Straight and Narrow Way," *Ensign*, November 1990, lds.org.
- Joseph B. Wirthlin, "The Abundant Life," *Ensign*, May 2006, lds.org.
- Joseph B. Wirthlin, "Sunday Will Come," *Ensign*, November, 2006, lds.org.

REFERENCES--WITNESSES OF THE SAVIOR'S BIRTH

- Marvin J. Ashton, "Come and See," *New Era*, December 1989, lds.org.
- Merrill J. Bateman, "A Season for Angels," *Ensign*, December 2007, lds.org.
- Erza Taft Benson, "The Savior's Visit to America," *Ensign*, May 1987, lds.org.
- Susan Easton Black, "Mary, His Mother," *Ensign*, January 1991, lds.org.
- Sue Clark, "The Star, the Savior, and our Heart," *New Era*, December 2008, lds.org.
- George Durrant, "I Found the Heart of Christmas," *Ensign*, December 1985, lds.org.
- Eric Huntsman, "Glad Tidings of Great Joy," *Ensign*, December 2010, lds.org.
- Henry B. Eyring, "The Gifts of Christmas," Christmas Devotional 2011, lds.org.
- David A. Bednar, "Converted unto the Lord," *Ensign*, November 2011, lds.org.
- Jeffrey R. Holland, "Christmas Comfort," Jeffrey R. Holland, @video.byui.edu/media
- Patrick Kearon, "Come, Let Us Adore Him," *Ensign*, December 2011, lds.org.
- Robert Matthews, "John the Baptist: A Burning and a Shining Light," *Ensign*, September 1972, lds.org.
- Robert Matthews, "Mary and Joseph," *Ensign*, December 1974, lds.org.
- Joseph F. McConkie, "Twelve Witnesses of Christ's Birth," *Ensign*, December 1990, lds.org.
- Thomas S. Monson, "A Bright Shining Star," lds.org/broadcast/article/christmas-devotional/2012/12/a-bright-shining-star?lang=eng
- Thomas S. Monson, "Preparing the Way," *Ensign*, May 1980. lds.org.
- Thomas S. Monson, "The Search for Jesus," *Ensign*, December 1990, lds.org.
- Thomas S. Monson, "True Shepherds," *Ensign*, November 2013, lds.org.
- Marvin J. Ashton, "Come and See," *New Era*, December 1989, lds.org.
- Annie Tintle, "In Shepherds Field," *Ensign*, December 2008, lds.org.
- Russell M. Nelson, "The Peace and Joy of Knowing the Savior Lives," *Ensign*, December 2011, lds.org.

- Dallin H. Oaks, "Witnesses of Christ," *Ensign*, November 1990, lds.org.
- Dieter F. Uchtdorf, "Of Curtains, Contentment, and Christmas," Christmas Devotional, December 2011, lds.org/broadcasts
- Susan Winters, "Mary and Joseph," *New Era*, December 2006, lds.org.

REFERENCES--DAILY SCRIPTURE

- *The Holy Bible King James Version.* The Church of Jesus Christ of Latter-day Saints, Salt Lake City, Utah, ©1979 Intellectual Reserve.

- *The Book of Mormon.* The Church of Jesus Christ of Latter-day Saints, Salt Lake City, Utah, ©1981 Intellectual Reserve.

REFERENCES--DAILY QUOTE

- Marvin J. Ashton, "Come and See," *New Era*, December 1989, lds.org. © By Intellectual Reserve, Inc.
- C. S. Lewis, *The Last Battle*, Bodley Head, London, 1956. (seventh volume—*The Chronicles of Narnia*)
- Gordon B. Hinckley, "The Wondrous and True Story of Christmas," *Ensign*, December 2000, lds.org. © By Intellectual Reserve, Inc.
- Laura Ingalls Wilder, *A Little House Sampler*, University of Nebraska Press, 1988.
- Anonymous, "Angels We Have Heard on High."
- Deiter F. Uchtdorf, "The Good and Grateful Receiver," Christmas Devotional 2012, lds.org/broadcasts. © By Intellectual Reserve, Inc.
- Charles Dickens, *A Christmas Carol*, Chapman & Hall, London, 1843.
- C.S. Lewis, *The Lion, the Witch, and the Wardrobe*, Geoffrey Bles, London, 1950.
- Patrick Kearon, "Come Let Us Adore Him," *Ensign*, December 2011, lds.org. © By Intellectual Reserve, Inc.
- Charles Dickens, *A Christmas Carol*, Chapman & Hall, London, 1843.
- John A. Widtsoe, "The Gifts of Christmas," *Ensign*, December 1972, lds.org © By Intellectual Reserve, Inc.
- Henry Wadsworth Longfellow, "I Heard the Bells on Christmas Day." Traditional Christmas Carol, based on a poem written in 1863.
- Dieter F. Uchtdorf, "Of Curtains, Contentment, and Christmas," Christmas Devotional, December 2011, lds.org/broadcasts. © By Intellectual Reserve, Inc.
- Henry van Dyke, "Keeping Christmas," *Six Days of the Week*, Charles Scribner's Sons. New York, 1924.
- Thomas S. Monson, "In Search of the Christmas Spirit," *Ensign*, December 1987, lds.org. © By Intellectual Reserve, Inc.
- Charles Dickens, *A Christmas Carol*, Chapman & Hall, London, 1843.

REFERENCES

- Benjamin Franklin, *Poor Richard's Almanac, 1743.*
- Howard W. Hunter, "The Real Christmas," *Ensign,* December 2005, lds.org. © By Intellectual Reserve, Inc.
- Charles Dickens, *A Christmas Carol,* Chapman & Hall, London, 1843.
- Gordon B. Hinckley, "The Wondrous and True Story of Christmas," *Ensign,* December 2000, lds.org. © By Intellectual Reserve, Inc.
- Phillips Brooks, "O Little Town Of Bethlehem."
- Hugh W. Pinnock, "Who Needs Christmas?" *New Era,* December 1987, lds.org. © By Intellectual Reserve, Inc.

Additional Resources

ADDITIONAL TIPS:

- Make your own version. Mix and match the music, books, stories, challenges/activities from various versions, for example I divided the costume version into several years making only one or two costumes each year. You may use the lists of books and stories provided in the Reference Section to come up with your own format. If you find one or more of the books, challenges, stories, or activities truly helpful, use it again the next year.

- Prioritize. This may be a time to ask yourself, "Does this help us act, remember, or be like Jesus?" If this activity does not answer this question, maybe it is time to change or eliminate it.

- Involve your family members, especially children old enough to help. Ask them to lead the night's events. Involve them in the music, books/stories and the activities, even the wrapping and planning.

- Make it personal. Add your testimony, have dad or grandpa record a story or book, and add inscriptions in the front cover of the books.

- Modified Family Home Evening version. If you find that your schedule does not permit you to do all the suggestions in the format you have chosen, pick four or five of the themes, and use them for Family Home Evenings.

- If you prefer, instead of purchasing each book, check your local library. Another great option are used books either online or at local used bookstores.

GRANDPARENT TIPS:

- You may need to use several different versions in a given year, depending on your children. Things to consider: age of the grandchildren, delivery method, preferences of the families, and any special needs.

- I chose to make this my only Christmas gift to my grandchildren. For this reason, I included additional gifts and personal treats. This also influenced my decision to wrap everything.

- It is especially important when doing this as a grandparent that you provide your children with a copy of your version. It will make it easier for them to coordinate their December.

- Remember to include the instruction page and any tips that might be helpful.

- You may want to discuss this gift with your children before proceeding.

- This is a gift to my grandchildren, and also my children so I like to include everything needed. By preparing everything in advance, December can be a fun and enriching month for all.

Items to Purchase or Prepare

ORIGINAL FAMILY VERSION

** Indicates Grandparent/Additional Gift Option

GENERAL DIRECTIONS

1. For stories, print and place in vinyl sheet covers or place in a 9" x12" envelope.
2. Label all items with corresponding character name.
3. Use gift bags to keep the day's items together.
4. Print instructions. Print a copy of the version you are using. Cut each character section into strips and include in gift bags. You may want to enclose the instructions in a card or envelope.

ITEMS USED EACH DAY

1. Select a Nativity set that includes Mary, Joseph, donkey, Three Wise Men, camel, shepherd, lamb, and Baby Jesus. Optional Items include: angel, star, manger, cow, and stable.
2. Purchase *Children's Songbook* and/or *Children's Songbook CD*, of The Church of Jesus Christ Latter-day Saints.

MANGER

1. Wrap manger (if separate from Baby Jesus)
2. Print Story, "Straw for the Manger," Jacob F. Frandsen
3. Construct a simple wooden manger, following the instructions in Additional Resources or substitute a small box or basket. **Fun project for grandpa
4. Make a simple doll representing Baby Jesus, instructions in the Additional Resources, or you may prefer to substitute a small baby doll. ** Fun for grandma.
5. Cut natural straw (colored raffia) into lengths to fit your manger
6. Optional: Prep all items for the manger and doll and get your children or grandchildren involved with this craft activity.

MARY

1. Wrap Mary figure
2. Purchase and wrap book---*Why Christmas Trees Aren't Perfect*, Richard H. Schneider
3. **Purchase gift for daughter or daughter-in-law, consider the book---*Mary, the Mother of Jesus* by Camille Fronk Olson
4. **Purchase gift-wrapping supplies that children can use to wrap their mother's present.

JOSEPH

1. Wrap Joseph figure
2. Find video on lds.org, "Joseph and Mary Travel to Bethlehem"
3. **Purchase Flannel Board & Nativity Flannel Board Characters (storytimefelts.com)

DONKEY

1. Wrap donkey figure
2. Purchase and wrap DVD or book—*The Little One*, Pamela Reid
3. **Purchase and wrap bird feeder and seeds

FIRST WISE MAN

1. Wrap one Wise Man figure
2. Purchase and wrap book—*The Carpenter's Gift*, David Rubel
3. **cookie/brownie mix, homemade or purchased

SECOND WISE MAN

1. Wrap Wise Man figure
2. Purchase and wrap—*Christmas Train*, Thomas S. Monson
3. Enclose one-dollar bill for each family member, with instructions in an envelope

THIRD WISE MAN

1. Wrap Wise Man figure
2. Purchase and wrap book—*The Tale of the Three Trees: A Traditional Folktale* retold by Angela Elwell Hunt
3. **Purchase and wrap craft supplies or kit to make three ornaments per child

CAMEL

1. Wrap camel figure
2. Print "The Littlest Camel" from Appendix
3. **Make or purchase a storyboard, instructions included in Additional Resources
4. **Purchase and wrap art supplies—white cardstock, markers, 8 1/2" × 11" vinyl sheet covers.

SHEPHERD

1. Wrap shepherd figure or figures
2. Purchase and wrap—*The Little Shepherd's Christmas*, Carol Heyer
3. Purchase and wrap—candy canes (minimum of 2 for each child)

LAMB

1. Wrap lamb figure or figures
2. Purchase and wrap book—*The Crippled Lamb,* Max Lucado
3. **Purchase and wrap pajamas for each child

BABY JESUS

1. Wrap Baby Jesus figure
2. **Purchase and wrap framed picture of Jesus Christ

OPTIONAL STABLE

1. Wrap stable if included in your set
2. **Purchase and wrap optional book—*The Story of Christmas, King James Bible,* Pamela Dalton
3. **Purchase—*The Story of Christmas Activity Book* or other Nativity activity book for each child

Items to Purchase or Prepare

CLASSIC CHILDREN'S LITERATURE VERSION

** Indicates Grandparent/Additional Gift Option

GENERAL DIRECTIONS

1. Label all items with corresponding character name.
2. Use gift bags to keep the day's items together.
3. If reusing Nativity figures from another version, you can either wrap them or just display the individual character while you are focusing on it.
4. Print instructions. Print a copy of this version. Cut each character section into strips and include in the gift bags. You may want to enclose the instructions in a card or envelope.

ITEMS USED EACH DAY

1. Nativity set
2. *Children's Songbook* and/or *Children's Songbook* CD

MANGER

1. Wrap manger from Nativity set
2. Cut raffia into lengths to fit your manger
3. Wrap manger and doll
4. **Purchase—*The Story of Christmas: from the King James Bible*, illustrated by Pamela Dalton or other illustrated Nativity book

ANGEL

1. Wrap angel figure
2. Purchase and wrap book—*This Is the Stable*, Cynthia Cotton
3. ** If your Nativity set did not include an angel, consider purchasing or using a separate angel. I chose to add a white porcelain angel with a small battery candle, which became a favorite for my grandchildren.

MARY

1. Wrap Mary figure
2. Purchase and Wrap book—*The Year of the Perfect Christmas Tree*, Gloria Houston
3. ** *"Christmas Box of Questions,"* (melissaanddoug.com)

JOSEPH

1. Wrap Joseph figure
2. Purchase and wrap book—*Christmas Day in the Morning*, Pearl S. Buck

DONKEY

1. Wrap donkey figure
2. Purchase and wrap book—*Mr. Willowby's Christmas*, Robert Barry

SHEPHERD

1. Wrap shepherd figure
2. Purchase and wrap book—*There Was No Snow on Christmas Eve*, Pam Munoz Ryan
3. **Purchase white pipe cleaners, borax, and string for making snowflakes

FIRST WISE MAN

1. Wrap wise man figure
2. Purchase and wrap book—*Christmas Miracle of Jonathan Toomey*, Susan Wojciechowski

SECOND WISE MAN

1. Wrap Wise Man figure
2. Purchase and Wrap Book—*The Gingerbread Doll*, Susan Tews, or if difficult to find, purchase *Christmas Tapestry*, Patricia Polacco
3. **A gingerbread cookie/house kit

CAMEL

1. Wrap camel figure
2. Purchase and wrap book—*The Christmas Star*, Marcus Pfister

THIRD WISE MAN

1. Wrap Wise Man figure
2. Purchase and wrap book—*The Man of the House at Huffington Row*, Mary Brigid Barrett, or if difficult to find, purchase *The Little Fir Tree*, Margaret Wise Brown

LAMB

1. Wrap lamb figure or figures
2. Purchase and wrap book—*Santa's Favorite Story, Santa Tells the Story of the First Christmas*, Husako Aoki
3. **Purchase and wrap "warm and wooly socks" for each family member

BABY JESUS

1. Wrap Baby Jesus figure

Items to Purchase or Prepare

COSTUME VERSION

** Indicates Grandparent/Additional Gift Option

GENERAL DIRECTIONS

1. Give costumes for each Nativity character. If you choose not to use the costumes, or to just do some costumes, you could continue to use a Nativity set as in previous years or give a new Nativity set. Puppets could also be used.

2. For stories, print and consider placing in vinyl sheet covers or placing in a 9" x12" envelope.

3. Label all items with corresponding character name.

4. Use gift bags to keep the day's items together.

5. If reusing Nativity figures from another version, you can either wrap them or display them.

6. Print instructions. Print a copy of this version. Cut each character section into strips and include in the gift bags. You may want to enclose the instructions in a card or envelope

ITEMS USED EACH DAY

1. *Children's Songbook* and/or CD from previous year

ANGEL

1. Make or purchase angel costume or wrap angel figure
2. Purchase and wrap—*The Story of Christmas---Storybook Set and Advent Calendar*, retold by Mary Packard---24 miniature books arranged in sequence and retelling the story of Christ's birth, along with an advent calendar
3. **Purchase a small Christmas tree for all the ornaments/books

MARY

1. Make or purchase Mary's costume or wrap Mary figure
2. Purchase and wrap book—*The Nativity Mary Remembers*, Laurie Knowlton, or if difficult to find, use the story, "Two Dimes and a Nickel," Richard A. Robb, *Ensign*, December 1986.
3. **Purchase restaurant gift card for their local area

JOSEPH

1. Make or purchase Joseph's costume or wrap Joseph figure
2. Purchase and wrap DVD—*Christmas for a Dollar*, Gale Sears
3. **Make and purchase treat for Dad

DONKEY

1. Make or purchase a prop or costume that could be used as a donkey in the Nativity play or wrap donkey figure
2. Purchase and wrap—*The Little Donkey*, Gerda Marie Scheidl, or if difficult to find, purchase *Christmas Farm*, Mary Lyn Ray
3. **Thank-you note cards and stamps

FIRST WISE MAN

1. Make or purchase a Wise Man costume or wrap Wise Man figure
2. Purchase and wrap book—*An Orange for Frankie*, Patricia Polacco
3. **Collect or purchase several hats, coats, or gloves to add to their donation

CAMEL

1. Make or purchase a costume or prop that could be used as a camel in the Nativity play or wrap camel figure
2. Purchase and wrap book—*The Last Straw*, Fredrick H. Thury

SECOND WISE MAN

1. Make or purchase a Wise Man costume or wrap Wise Man figure
2. Purchase and wrap—*Dressing-Up Sticker Book: Nativity Play,* illustrated by Kay Widdowson
3. **Sticker book

THIRD WISE MAN

1. Make or purchase a Wise Man costume or wrap Wise Man figure
2. Print Story—"Doll Brings Lesson on Christmas," Adrianna Cabello
3. **Purchase and wrap doll/animal sewing kit

SHEPHERD

1. Make or purchase a shepherd costume or wrap shepherd figure or figures
2. Purchase and wrap book—*The Little Shepherd Girl*, Juliann Henry

LAMB

1. Make or purchase a lamb costume or prop that could be used in the Nativity play or wrap lamb figure or figures
2. Purchase and wrap book—*The Scallop Christmas*, Jane Freeberg
3. **Purchase and wrap fleece fabric that has been cut into blanket sizes

BABY JESUS

1. Make or purchase swaddling clothes or wrap Baby Jesus figure

Items to Purchase or Prepare

TRADITIONAL CHRISTMAS CAROL VERSION

** Indicates Grandparent/Additional Gift Option

GENERAL DIRECTIONS

1. Select a traditional Christmas songbook to use. Choose one that suits the musical abilities of each family
2. For stories, print and consider placing in vinyl sheet covers, or placing in a 9" x12" Envelope.
3. Label all items with corresponding character name.
4. Use gift bags to keep the day's items together.
5. If reusing Nativity figures from another version, you can either wrap them or just display them.
6. Print instructions. Print a copy of this version. Cut each character section into strips and include in the gift bags. You may want to enclose the instructions in a card or envelope

ITEMS USED EACH DAY

1. Reuse Nativity set from previous year, or purchase a new set
2. Bells or chimes, optional
3. **Bells and/or chimes and would make a fun addition to this version. Another gift could be a Christmas songbook.

STABLE

1. Wrap stable, if included in your set
2. Purchase and wrap book—*Away in a Manger*, Mike Jaroszko

MARY

1. Wrap Mary figure
2. Purchase and wrap book—*Gifts of the Heart*, Patricia Polacco

DONKEY

1. Wrap donkey figure
2. Purchase and wrap book—*The Friendly Beasts*, Tomie dePaola (numerous editions of this carol are available with various illustrators)

COW

1. Wrap Cow figure
2. Purchase and wrap book—*The Boy of the Bells*, Carly Simon, or if difficult to find, *Jacobs Gift*, Max Lucado.

JOSEPH

1. Wrap Joseph figure
2. Print and wrap story—"A Helping Angel," Mary Joanne Steck
3. **Purchase and enclose a gift card for Dad (car wash or sporting goods, etc.)

FIRST WISE MAN

1. Wrap Wise Man figure
2. Purchase and wrap book—*We Three Kings*, illustrated by Gennady Spirin
3. **Collect gently used books to add to your children's collection to donate

SECOND WISE MAN

1. Wrap Wise Man figure
2. Locate video on lds.org and have ready to play
3. ** Make homemade Christmas candy & and wrap

THIRD WISE MAN

1. Wrap Wise Man figure
2. Purchase and wrap—--*The First Noel*, illustrated by Jody Wheeler
3. **Purchase hot chocolate mix or gift card for hot chocolate

CAMEL

1. Wrap camel figure
2. Purchase and wrap—*Good King Wenceslas*, illustrated by Omar Rayyan

SHEPHERD

1. Wrap shepherd figure
2. Purchase and wrap book—*The Little Drummer Boy*, Ezra Jack Keats
3. **Purchase children's drums or a children's musical instrument set

LAMB

1. Wrap lamb figure or figures
2. Purchase and wrap book—*The Littlest Camel and Other Christmas Stories*, Bob Hartman, "The Little Lambs" is one of the stories and is also available on iTunes
3. **Purchase and wrap—Nativity finger puppets

BABY JESUS

1. Wrap Baby Jesus figure
2. **Attend "Musical Evening"

Items to Purchase or Prepare

INTERFAITH VERSION

** Indicates Grandparent/Additional Gift Option

GENERAL DIRECTIONS

1. For stories, print and consider placing in vinyl sheet covers, or placing in a 9" x 12" envelope.
2. Label all items with corresponding character name.
3. Use gift bags to keep the day's items together.
4. Nativity Set—including angel, Mary, Joseph, donkey, shepherd, lamb, 3 Wise men, camel, and Baby Jesus
5. Print instructions. Print a copy of this version. Cut each character section into strips and include in the gift bags. You may want to enclose the instructions in a card or envelope.

ITEMS USED EACH DAY

1. Nativity set

ANGEL

1. Wrap angel figure
2. Purchase and wrap book—*The Sparkle Box*, Jill Hardie

MARY

1. Wrap Mary figure
2. Find story and prepare —"A Gift of the Heart," Norman Vincent Peale
3. **Purchase newborn baby clothes

JOSEPH

1. Wrap Joseph figure
2. **Purchase Christmas DVD and popcorn treat that Dad would like

DONKEY

1. Wrap donkey figure
2. Purchase and wrap book—*Room for a Little One*, Martin Waddell

LAMB

1. Wrap lamb figure or figures
2. Purchase and wrap book—*Angela and the Baby Jesus*, Frank McCourt
3. Make dinner, and take it to someone
4. **Make or purchase children's Christmas aprons

SHEPHERD

1. Wrap Shepherd figure or figures
2. Purchase and wrap book—*The Candymaker's Gift*, David and Helen Haidle
3. Purchase and wrap candy canes
4. **Purchase and wrap book—*A Christmas Manger, A Punch and Play Book*, H.A. Rey

FIRST WISE MAN

1. Wrap Wise Man figure
2. Purchase and wrap book—*Boxes for Katje*, Candace Fleming
3. **Purchase prepaid USPS mail package
4. **Purchase Christmas candy or other items to be included in the package

SECOND WISE MAN

1. Wrap Wise Man figure
2. Purchase and wrap book—*The Legend of the Poinsettia*, Tomie dePaola
3. **Purchase 2 poinsettia plants, one for your children/grandchildren and one for them to give away.

THIRD WISE MAN

1. Wrap Wise Man figure
2. Print Story—"Nellie's Gift," Anonymous (Appendix)
3. **Money jar and some coins

CAMEL

1. Wrap camel figure
2. Purchase and wrap book—*Humphrey's First Christmas*, Carol Heyer

BABY JESUS

1. Wrap Baby Jesus figure
2. **Purchase and wrap optional book—*The First Christmas, The King James Version*, illustrated by Jan Pienkowski
3. **Purchase and wrap Christmas box, include your special reminder of Christ to share with your grandchildren/children

MANGER ASSEMBLY – CAN BE
USED AS TEMPLATES

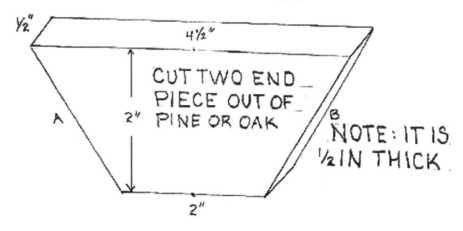

½"
4½"
CUT TWO END
PIECE OUT OF
PINE OR OAK
A
2"
B
NOTE: IT IS
½ IN THICK
2"

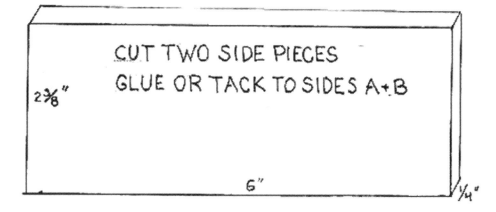

CUT TWO SIDE PIECES
GLUE OR TACK TO SIDES A + B
2⅜"
6"
¼"

CUT BOTTOM PIECE AND
GLUE OR TACK TO BASE
2"
6"
¼"

MAKE TWO CROSSING SUPPORT PIECES
AND GLUE THEM CROSS WISE ON THE
BASE – PAINT OR STAIN IF DESIRED

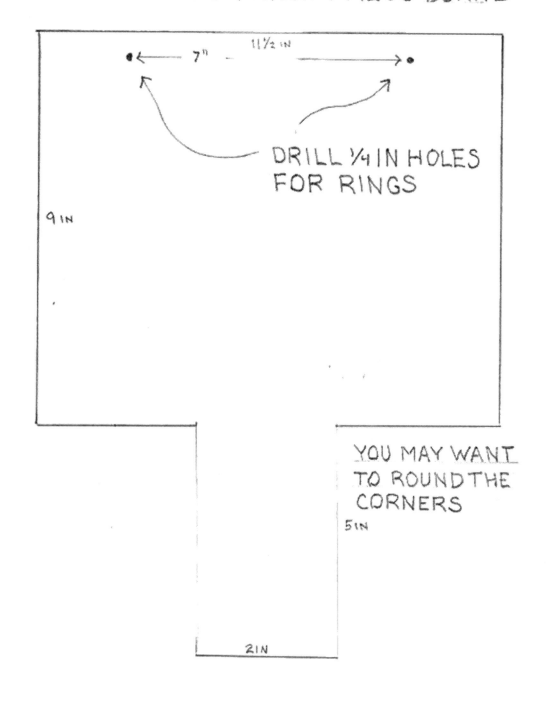

STORYBOARD
CUT FROM A 11½ × 14 INCH PRESS BOARD

11½ IN

7"

DRILL ¼ IN HOLES
FOR RINGS

9 IN

YOU MAY WANT
TO ROUND THE
CORNERS

5 IN

2 IN

DOLL INSTRUCTIONS

SUPPLIES

1. Lightweight cream-colored fabric—8" × 8" square
2. White flannel fabric—8" × 8" square
3. Thread
4. Batting—small amount to stuff doll
5. Black craft paint or fine-point permanent marker
6. Blush powder
7. Curly doll hair—available at craft stores
8. Glue—for attaching doll hair
9. Natural-colored twine—18"

DOLL INSTRUCTIONS

1. Using pattern for doll, cut out (2) pieces from the cream-colored fabric.
2. Sew the (2) pieces together using a ¾" seam. Sew down and around the three sides, leaving the bottom open. Carefully clip the rounded edges to prevent puckering.
3. Firmly stuff the doll.
4. Stitch across the bottom edge—I use a zigzag stitch to secure the edge.
5. Using a Q-tip, make (2) dots with the black paint for eyes (or use permanent marker.)
6. Use a small amount of blush on a cotton ball to color cheeks.
7. Glue a few strands of "curly doll hair" to the top of the doll.

SWADDLING CLOTH INSTRUCTIONS

1. Fold one corner of the white flannel square into square about 3½ inches.
2. Place the doll face down, a little below the eyes.
3. Fold one side in and tuck under doll.
4. Fold bottom corner up about 2 inches, and fold again at the bottom of the doll.
5. Fold the remaining edge around to the front of the doll.
6. Tie the twine around the middle of the doll, and tie a bow. Cut off any excess twine.

BORAX SNOWFLAKES

SUPPLIES

1. White pipe cleaners
2. String
3. Pencil
4. Jar—wide mouth
5. Borax
6. Boiling water
7. Blue food coloring (optional)

STEPS

1. Twist three 5-inch pieces of pipe cleaner together in the center.
2. For a more elaborate snowflake, twist an additional 1½" piece to each point.
3. Tie a piece of string to one end of the pencil. Tie the other end to a pencil.
4. Adjust the string so the pencil hangs the snowflake into the jar. Choose a large enough jar so the suspended snowflake doesn't touch the sides of the jar.
5. Fill the jar with at least 1 cup of boiling water. Add 1 tablespoon of borax. Stir to dissolve. Continue adding borax 1 tablespoon at a time until you have added 3 tablespoons for each cup of boiling water.
6. Optional: add 1 drop of blue food coloring if desired.
7. Hang the snowflake in the jar so the snowflake is completely covered with the liquid and hangs without touching the bottom or sides of the jar.
8. Let your snowflake sit in the liquid overnight for the crystals to form. Remove.
9. Hang your snowflake on your tree or in a window where it will catch the light.